THIS BOOK BELONGS TO:

____

COLOR TEST

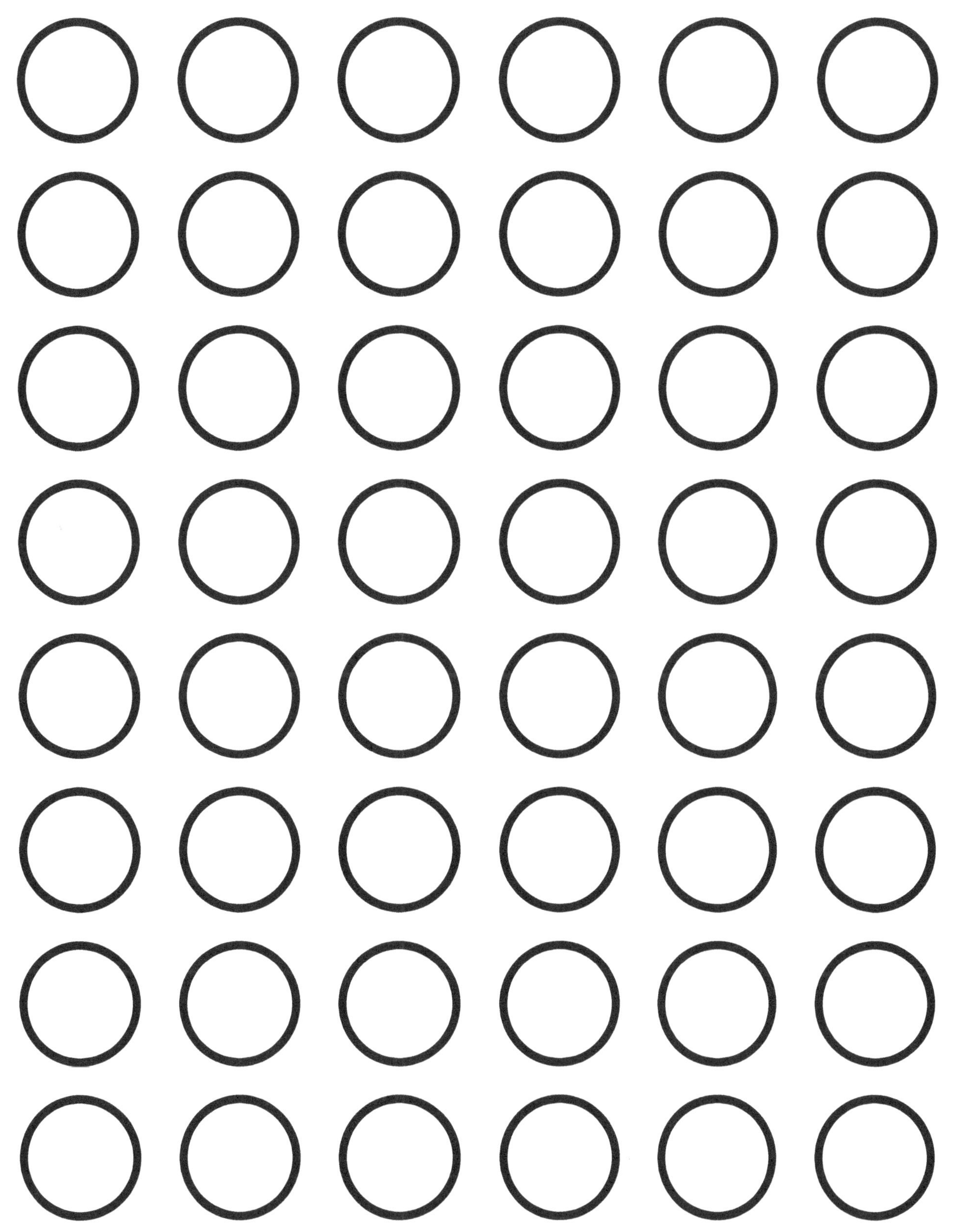

SOUTHERN HAWKER
Aeshna cyanea

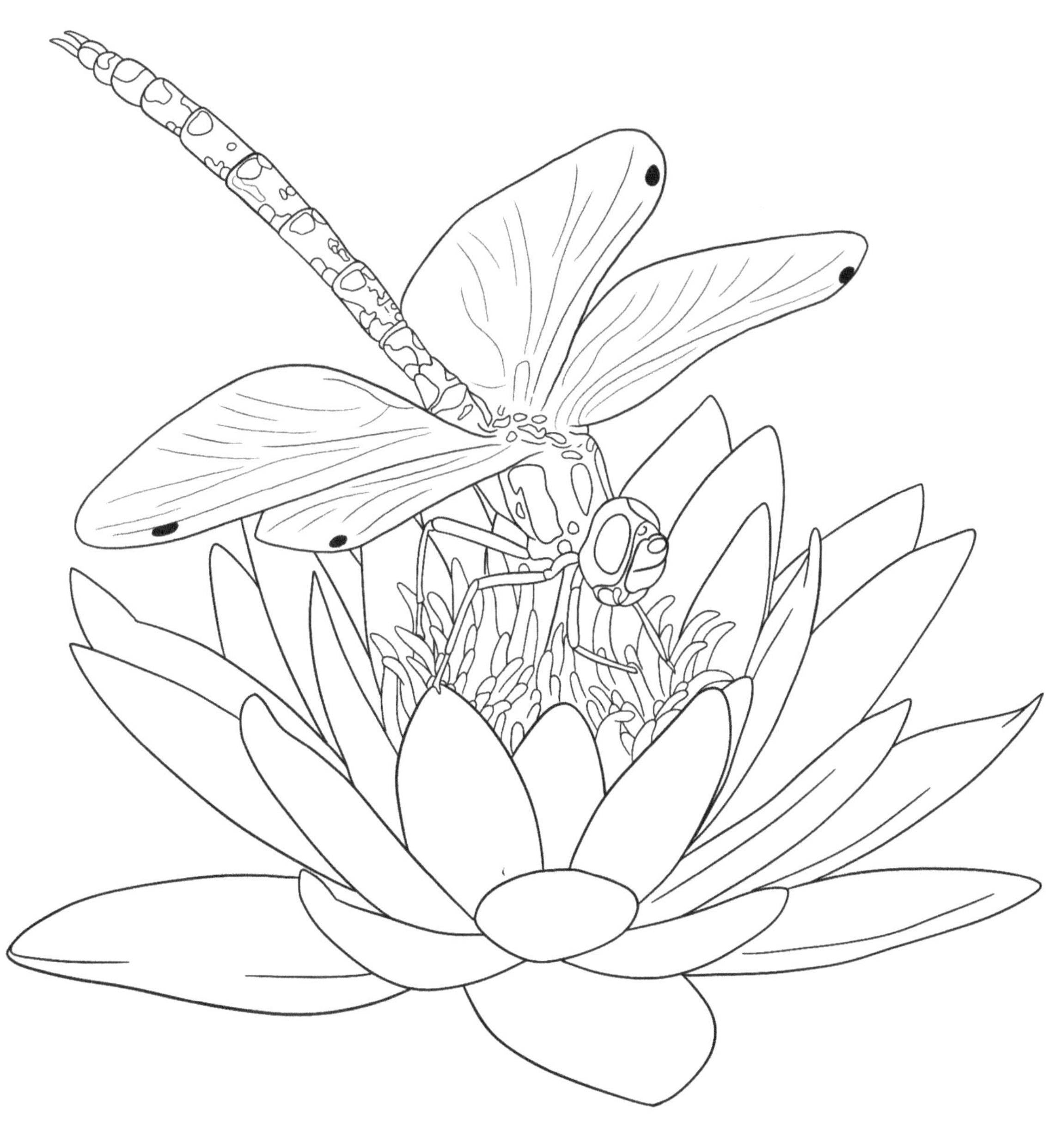

CECROPIA MOTH
Hyalophora cecropia

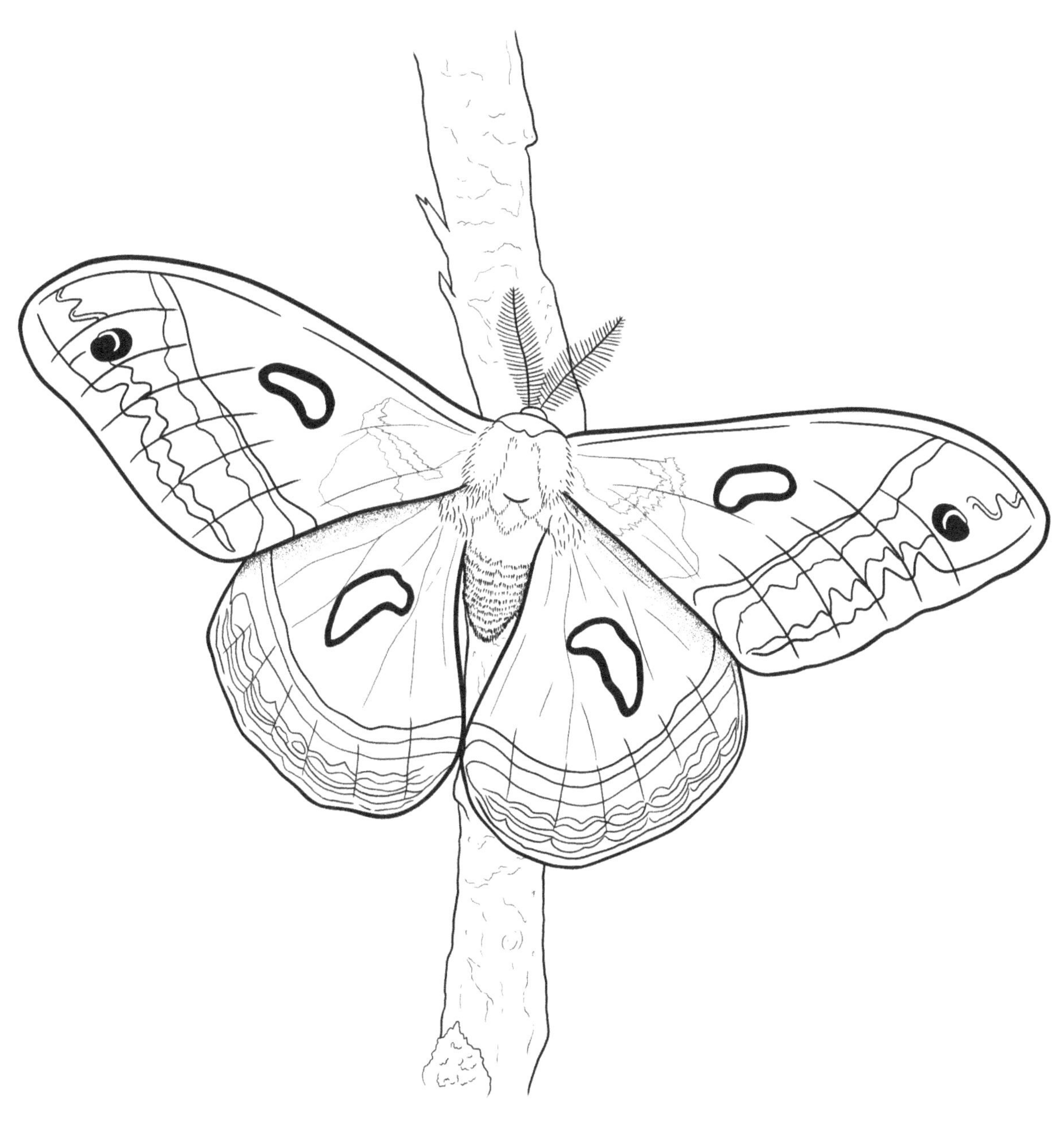

BURGUNDY SNAIL

Helix pomatia

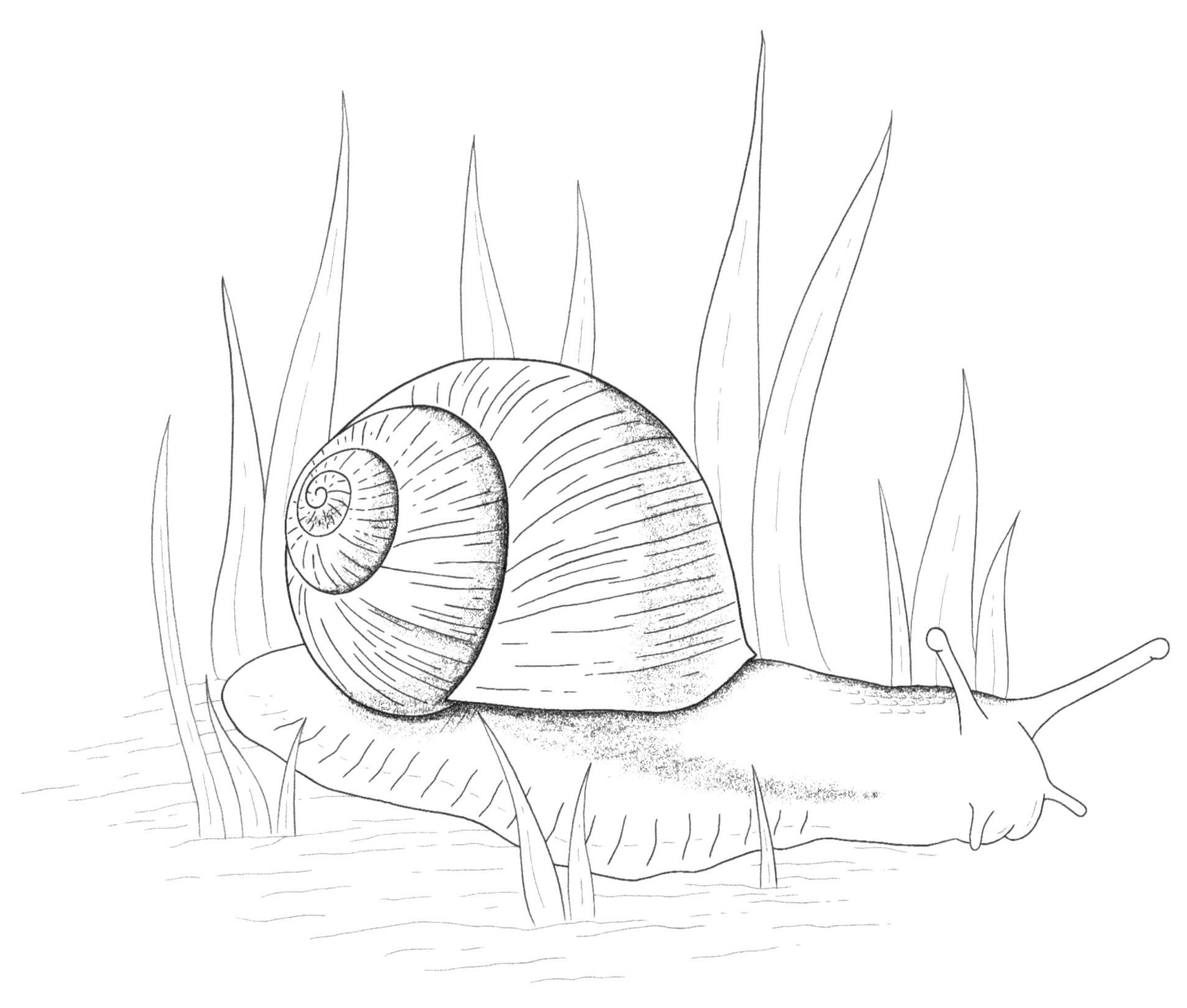

POND SLIDER

Trachemys scripta

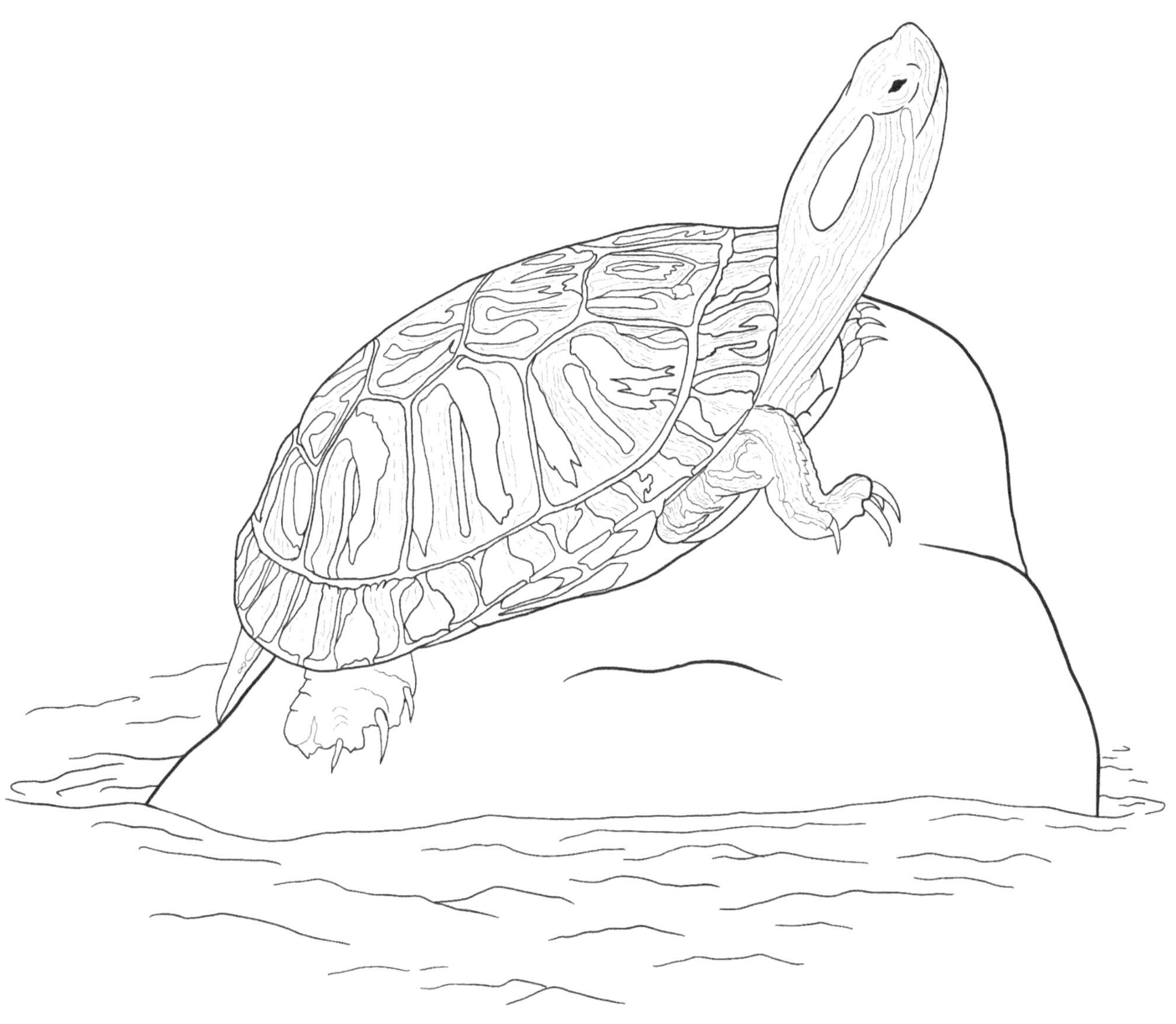

AMERICAN BIRD GRASSHOPPER

Schistocerca americana

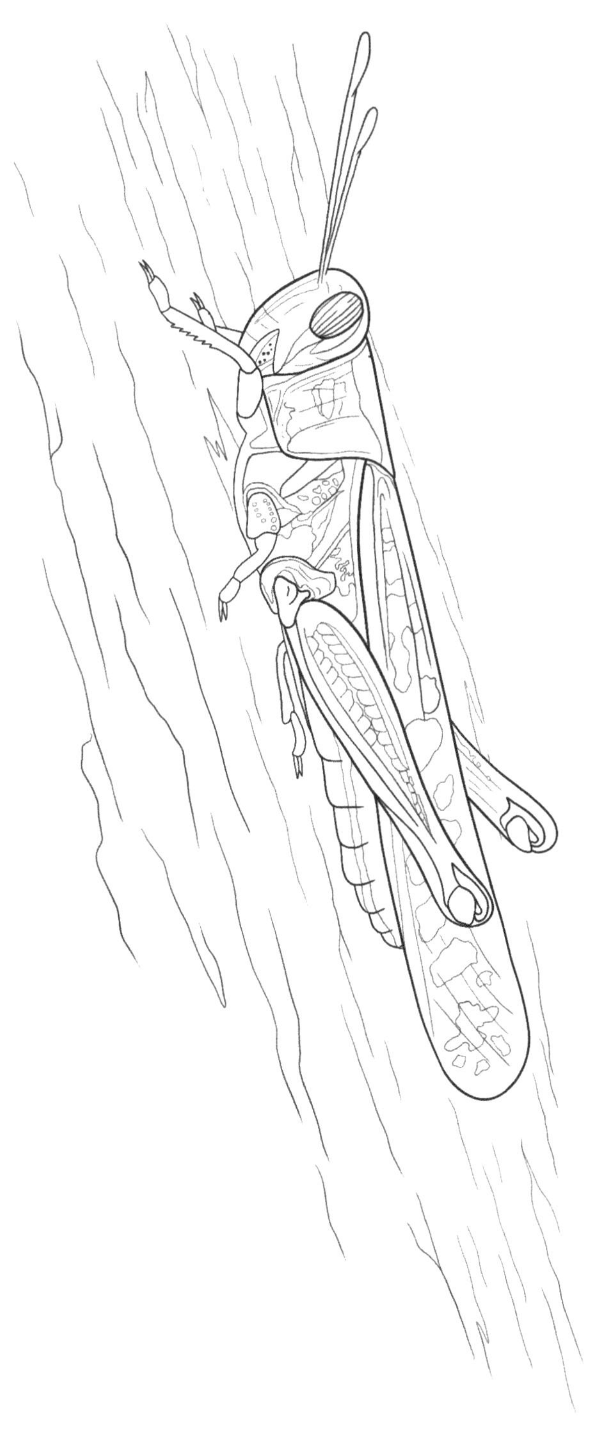

JAPANESE BEETLE
Popillia japonica

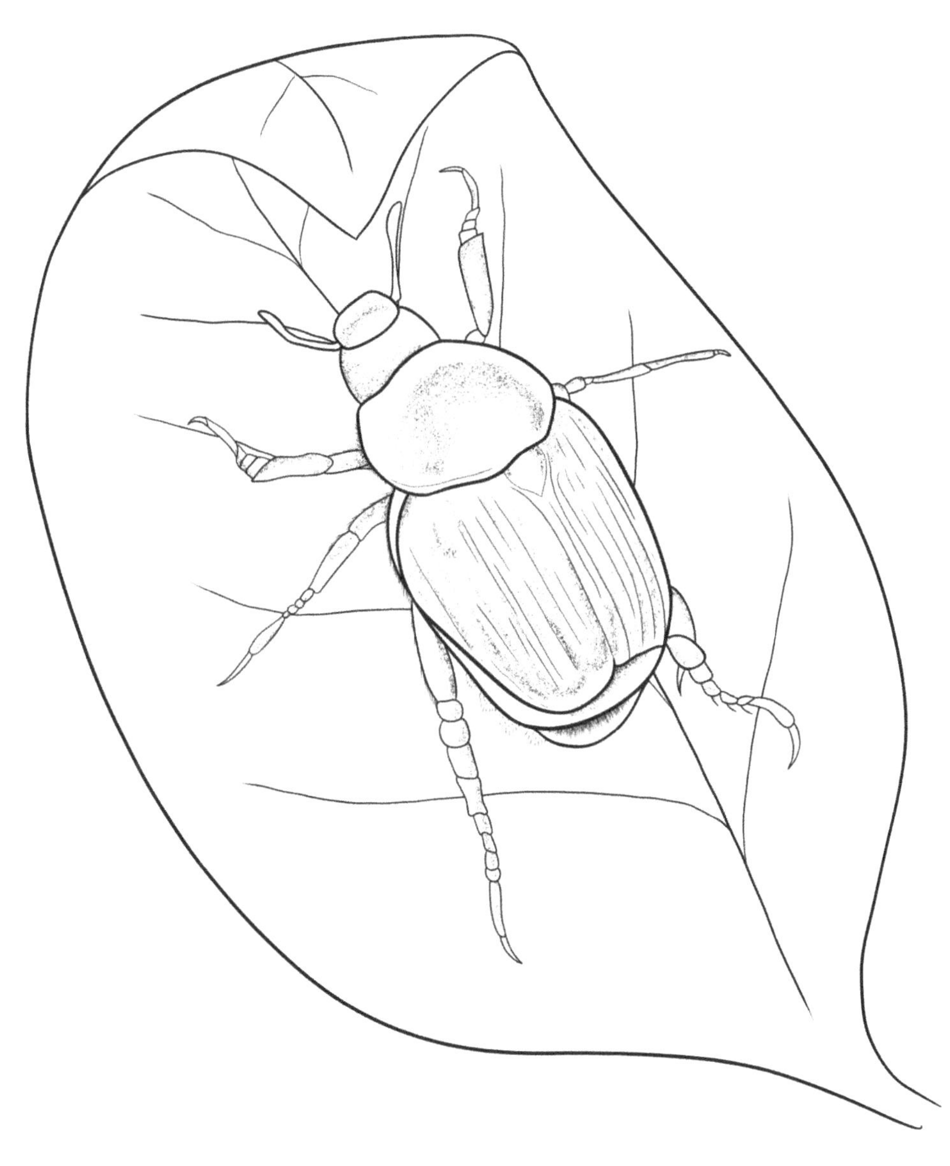

LUNA MOTH
Actias luna

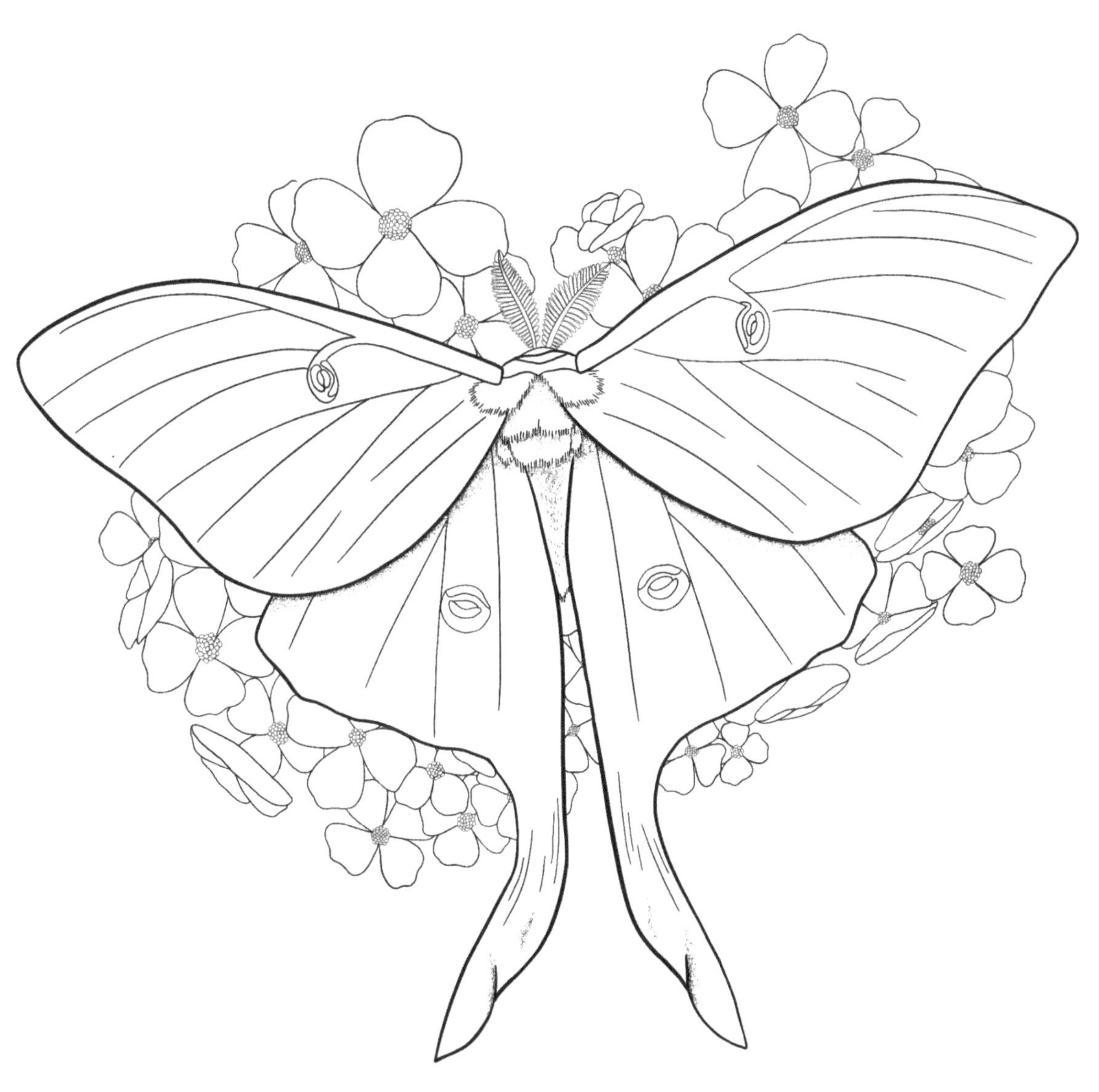

COMMON BLUE DAMSELFLY
Enallagma cyathigerum

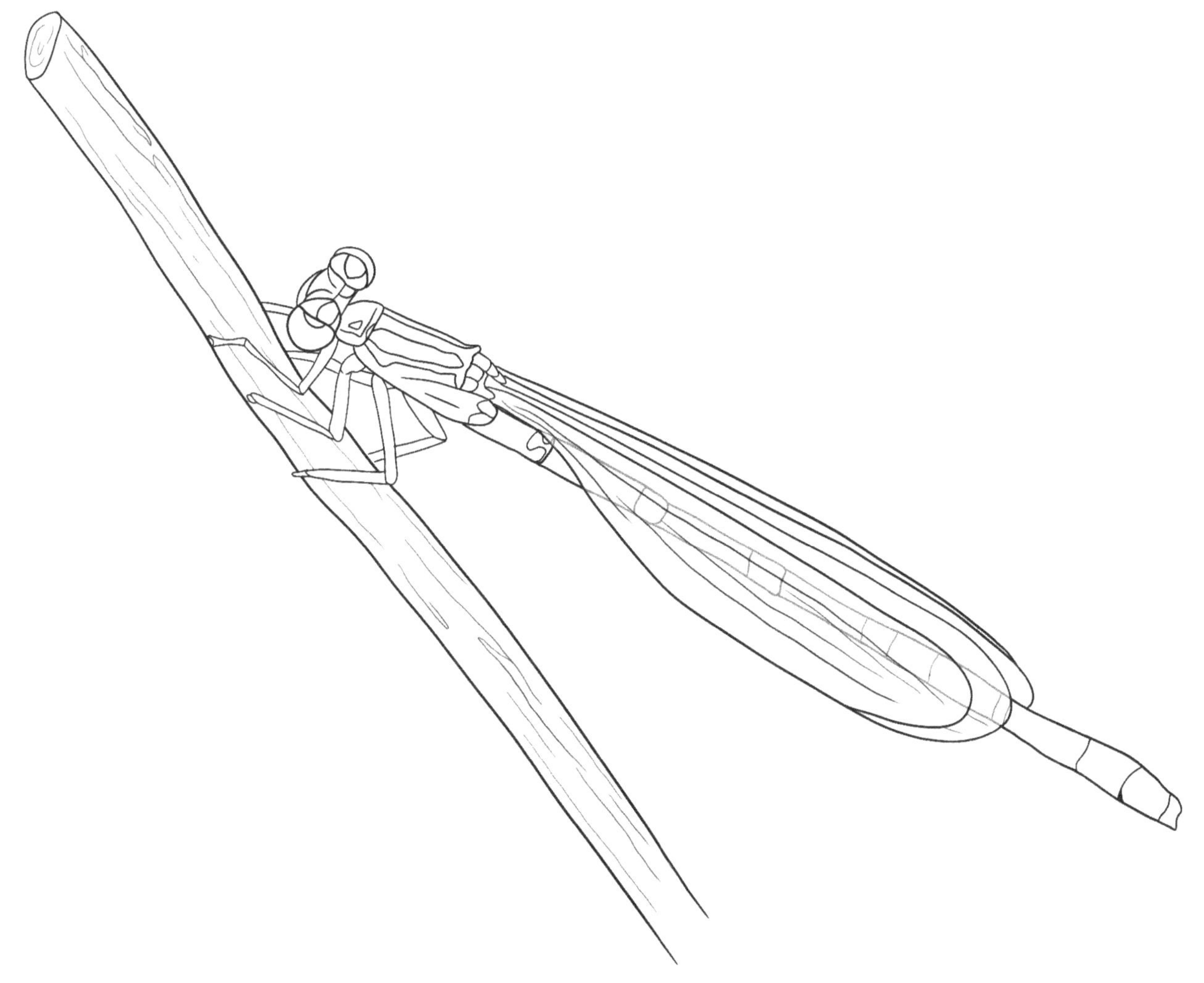

FIRE BELLY TOAD
Bombina bombina

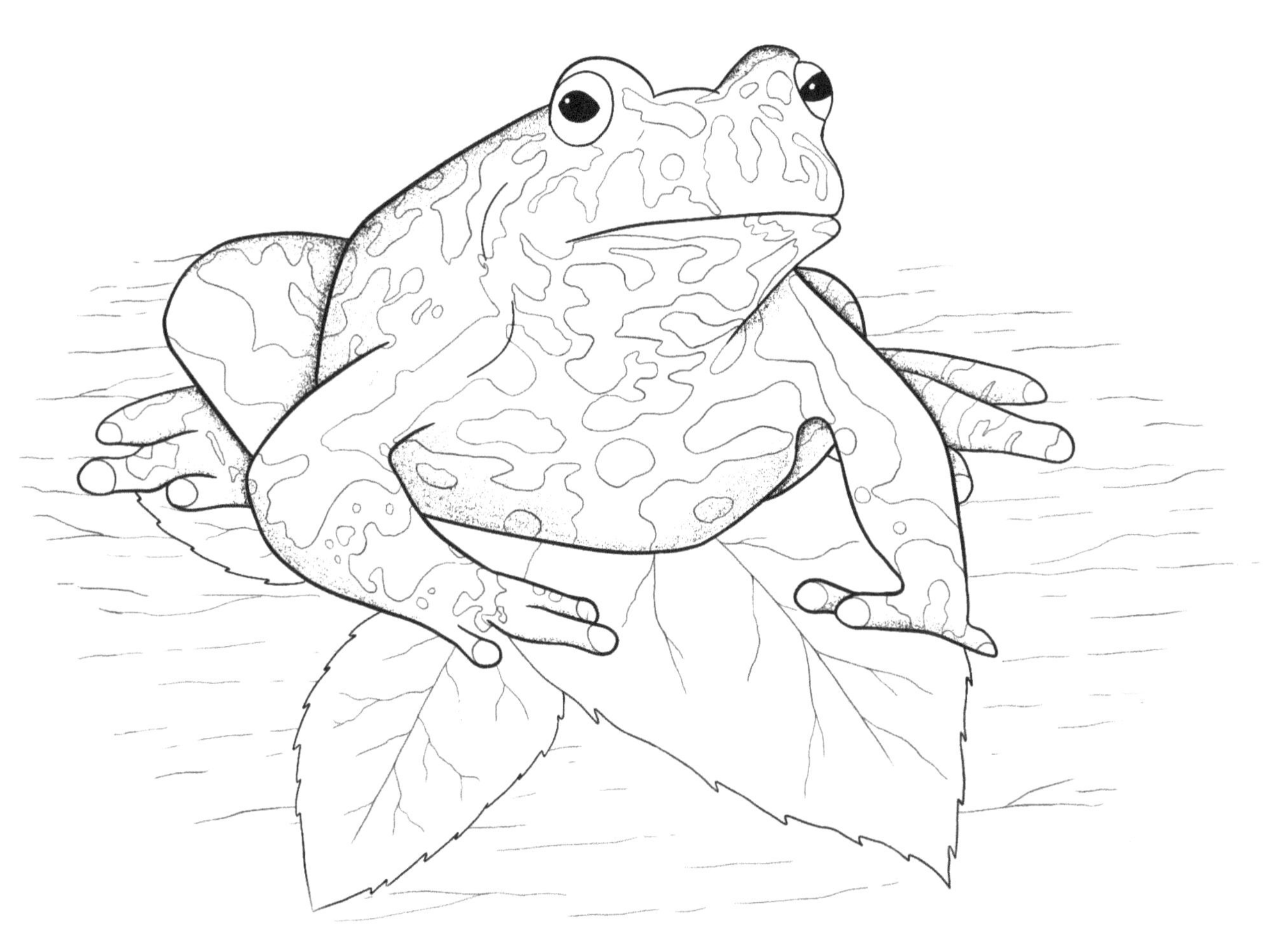

PAINTED LADY

Vanessa cardui

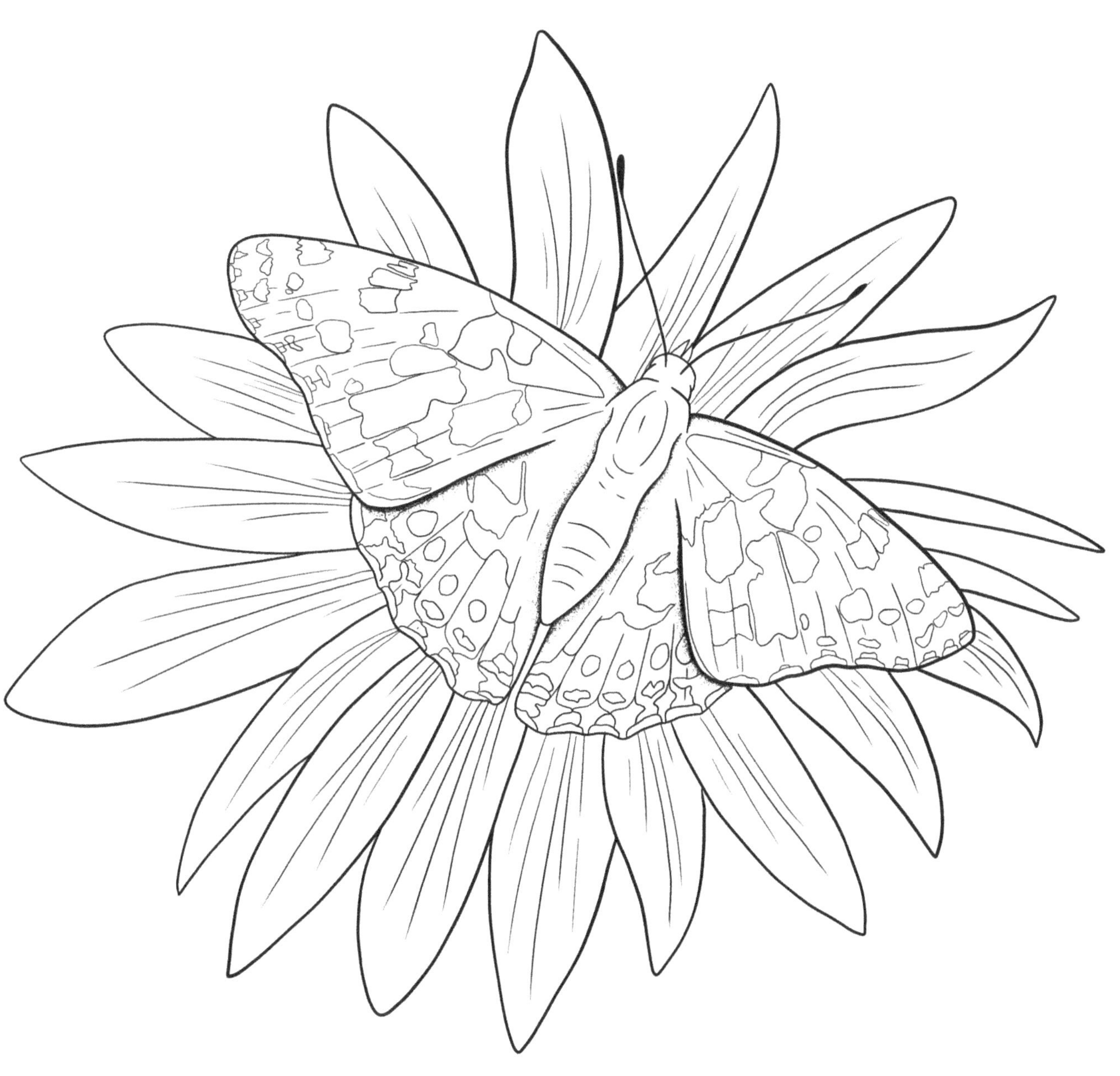

EASTERN LUBBER GRASSHOPPER

Romalea microptera

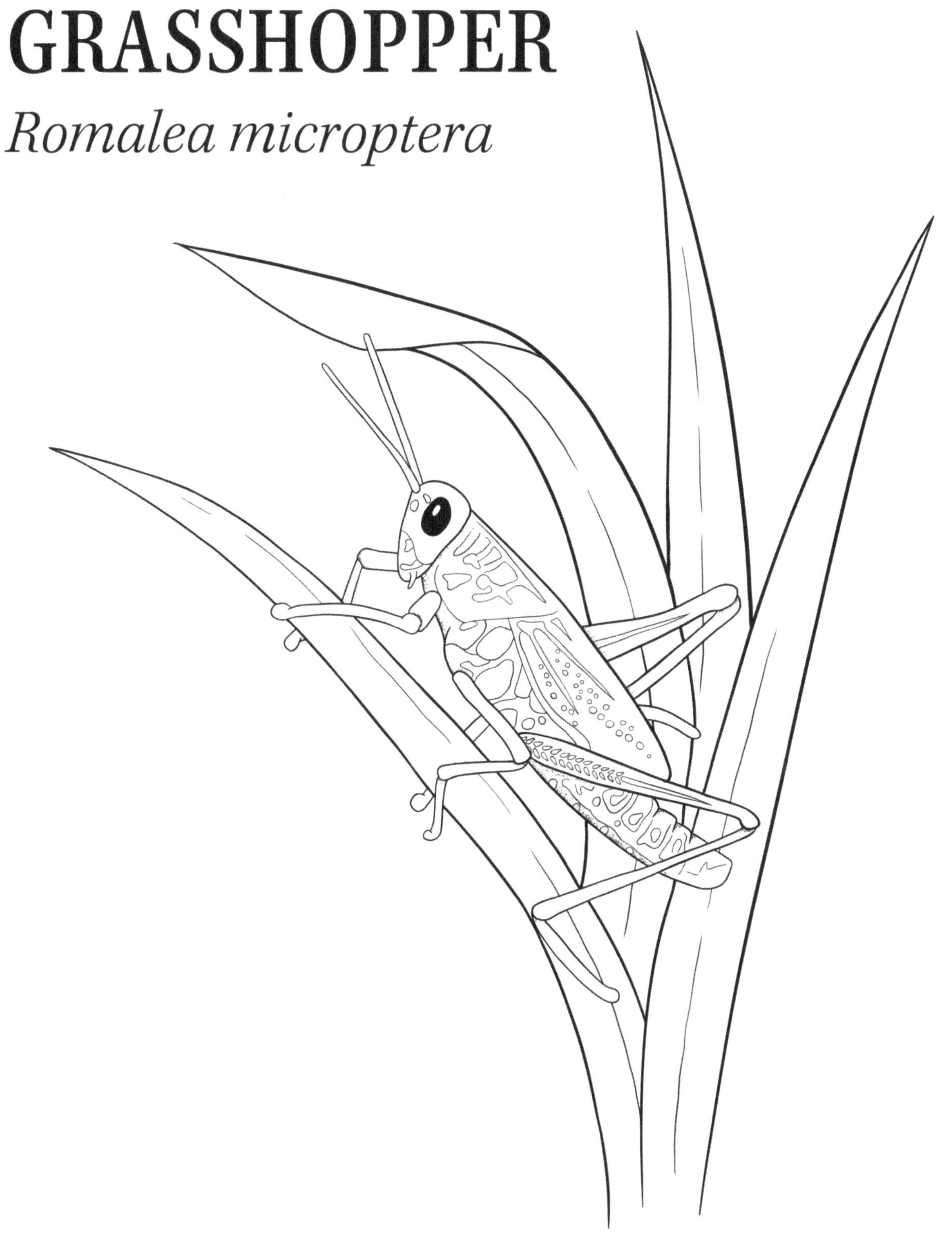

LADY BUG
Coccinellidae

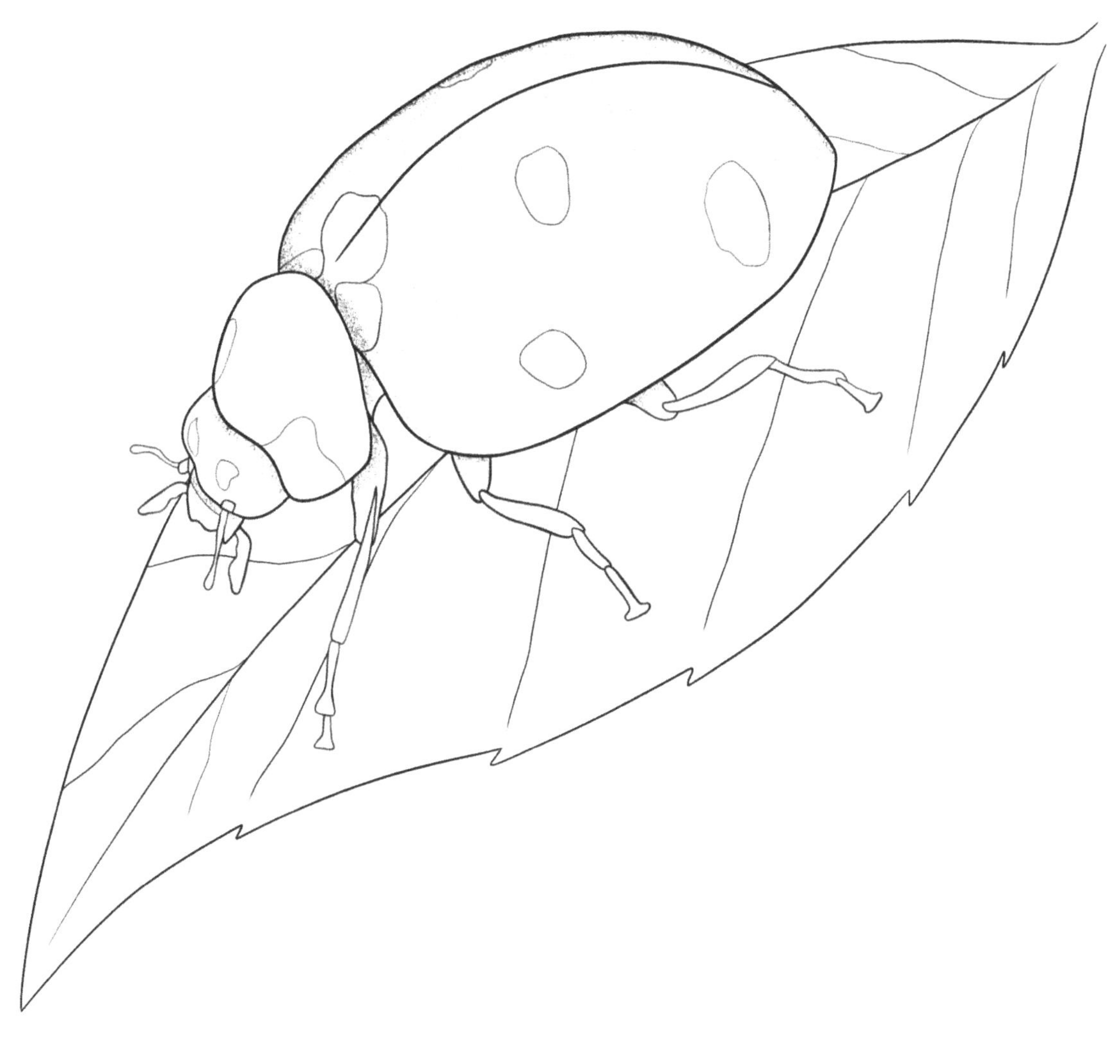

ATLAS MOTH
Attacus atlas

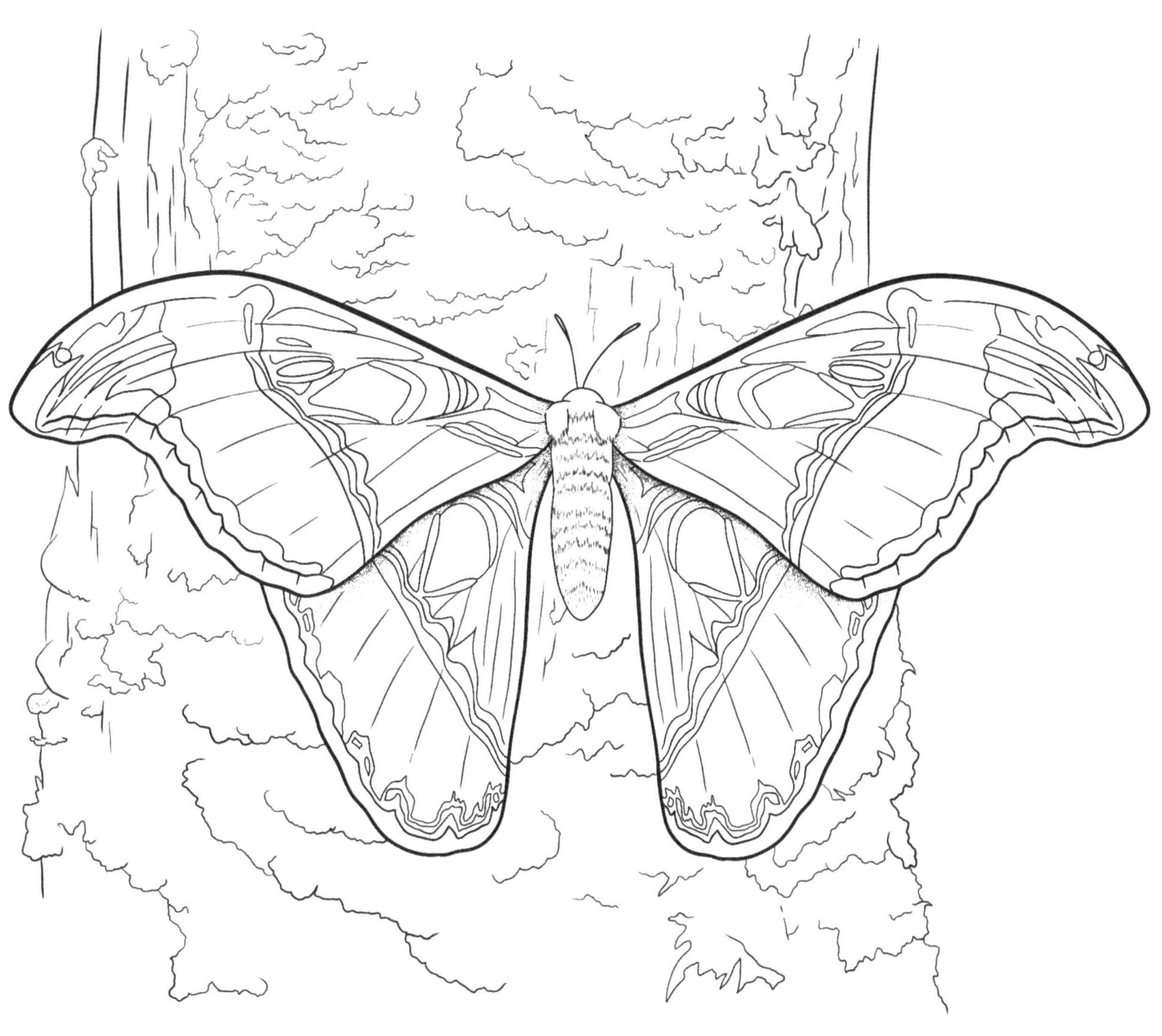

BUMBLE BEE
Bombus

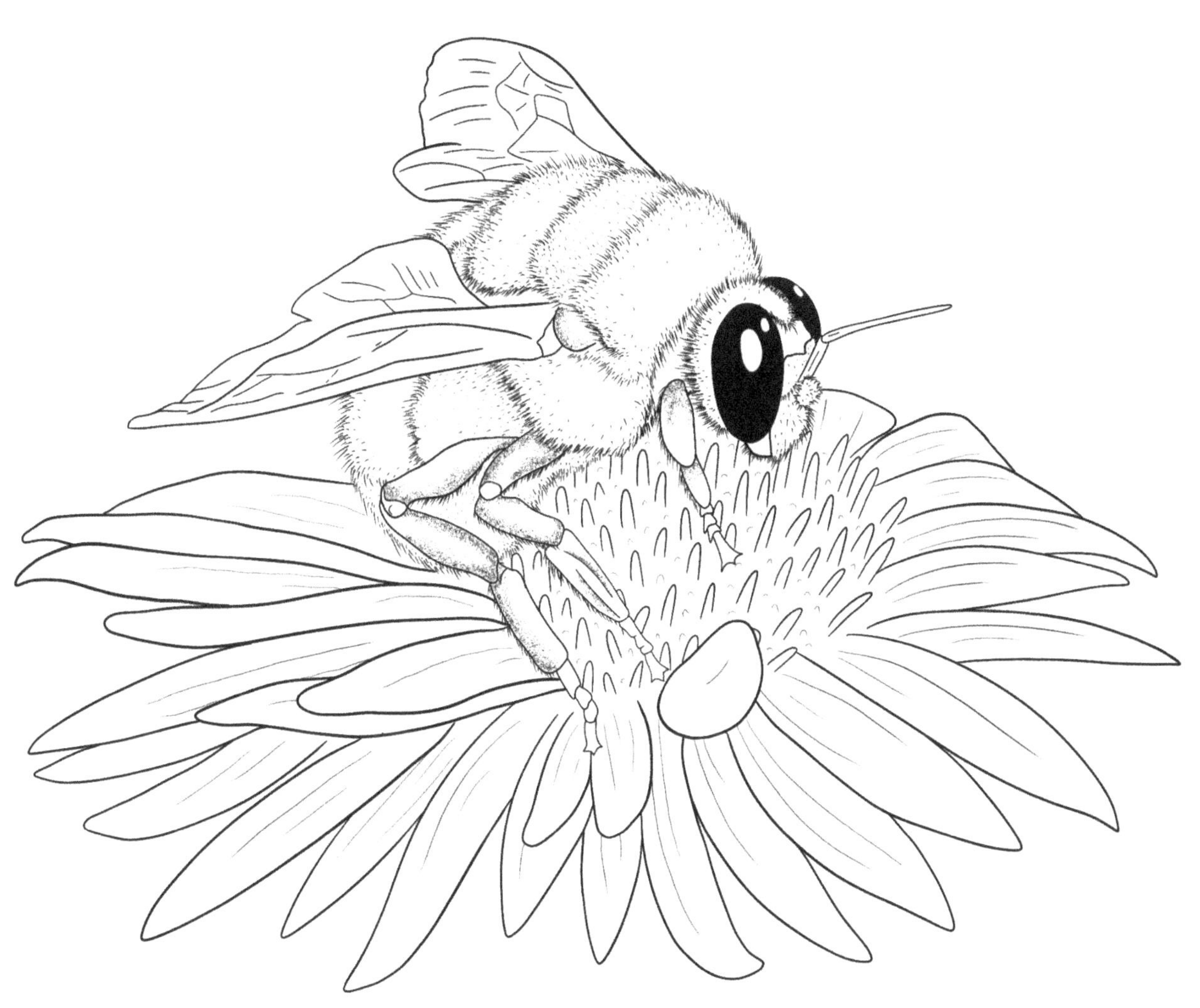

GREEN TREEFROG
Hyla cinerea

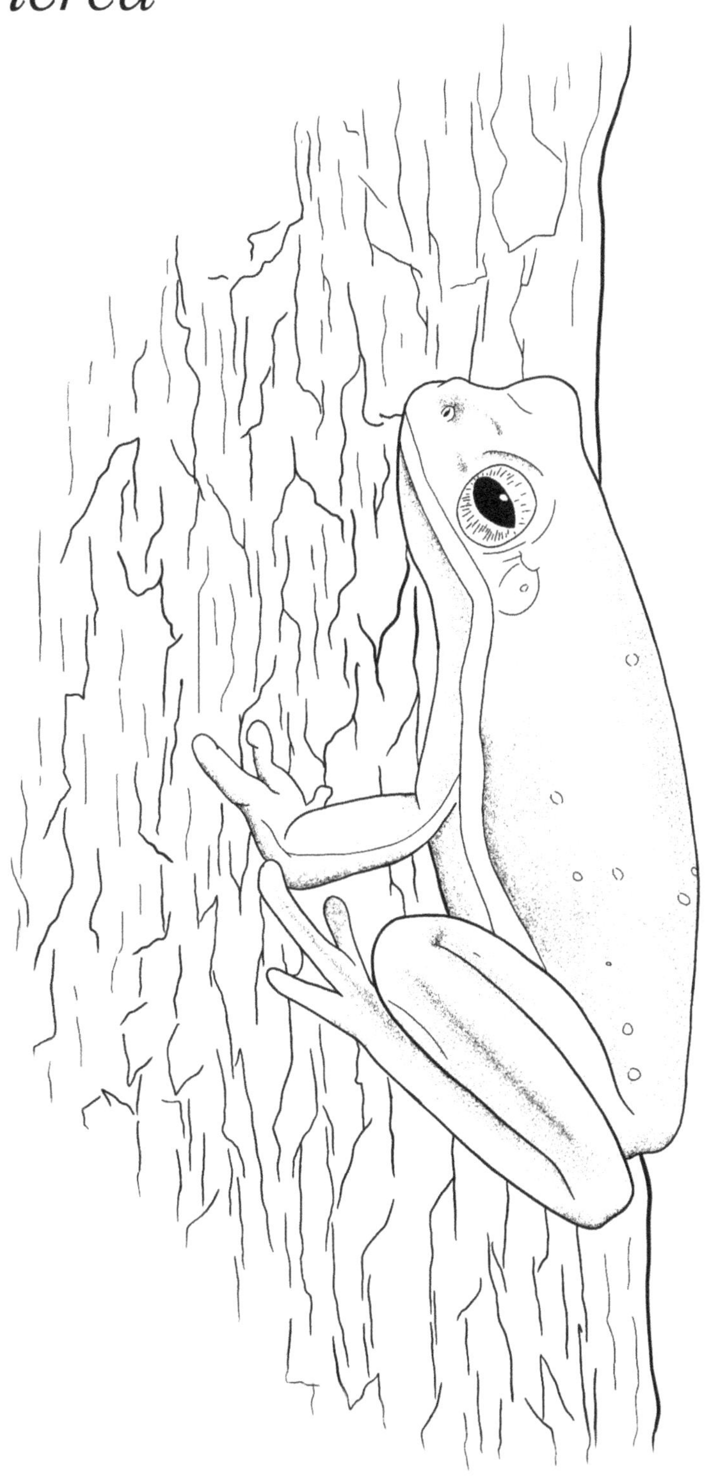

REGAL MOTH
Citheronia regalis

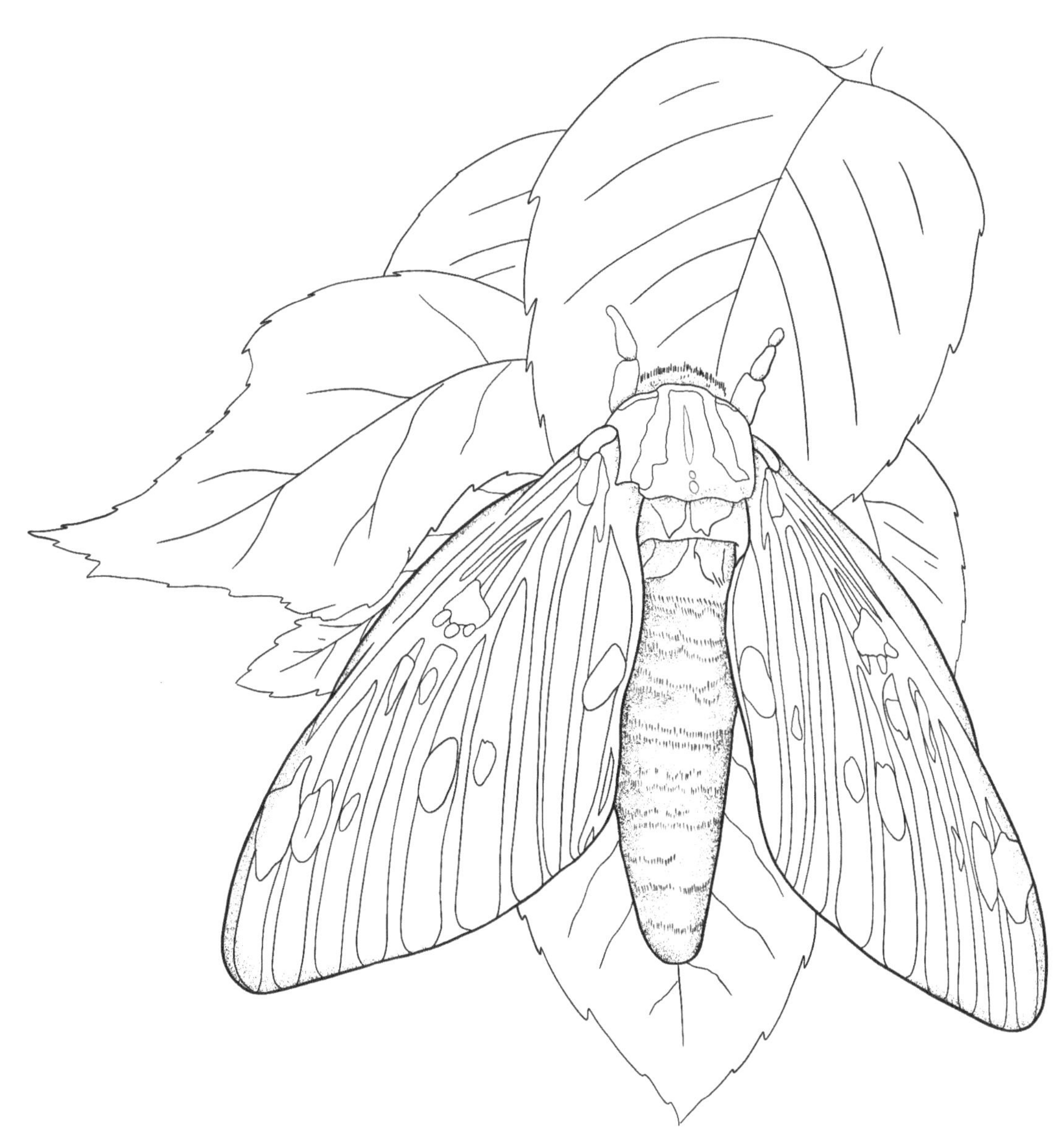

GNORMAN

Garden gnome

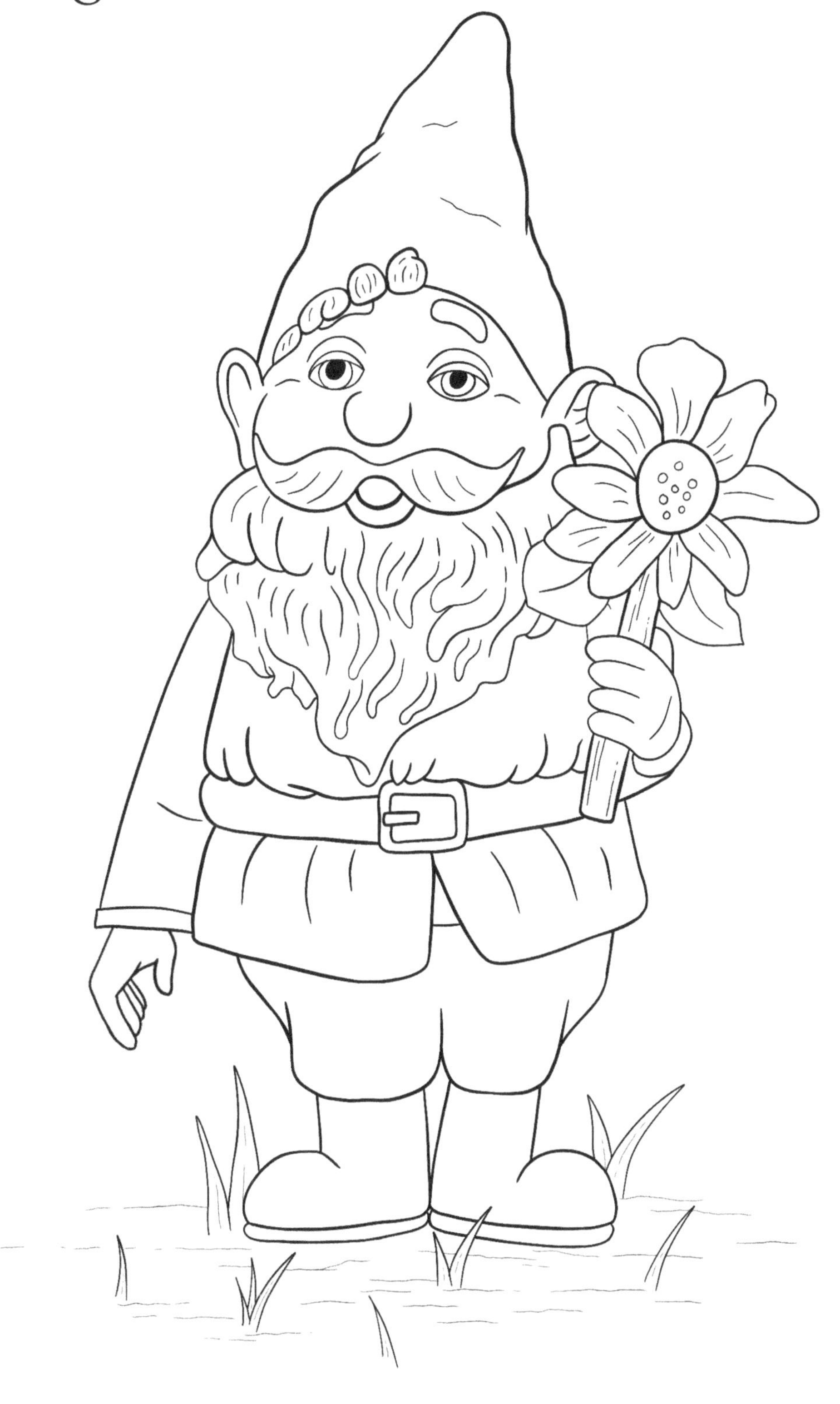

ANNUAL CICADA
Neotibicen canicularis

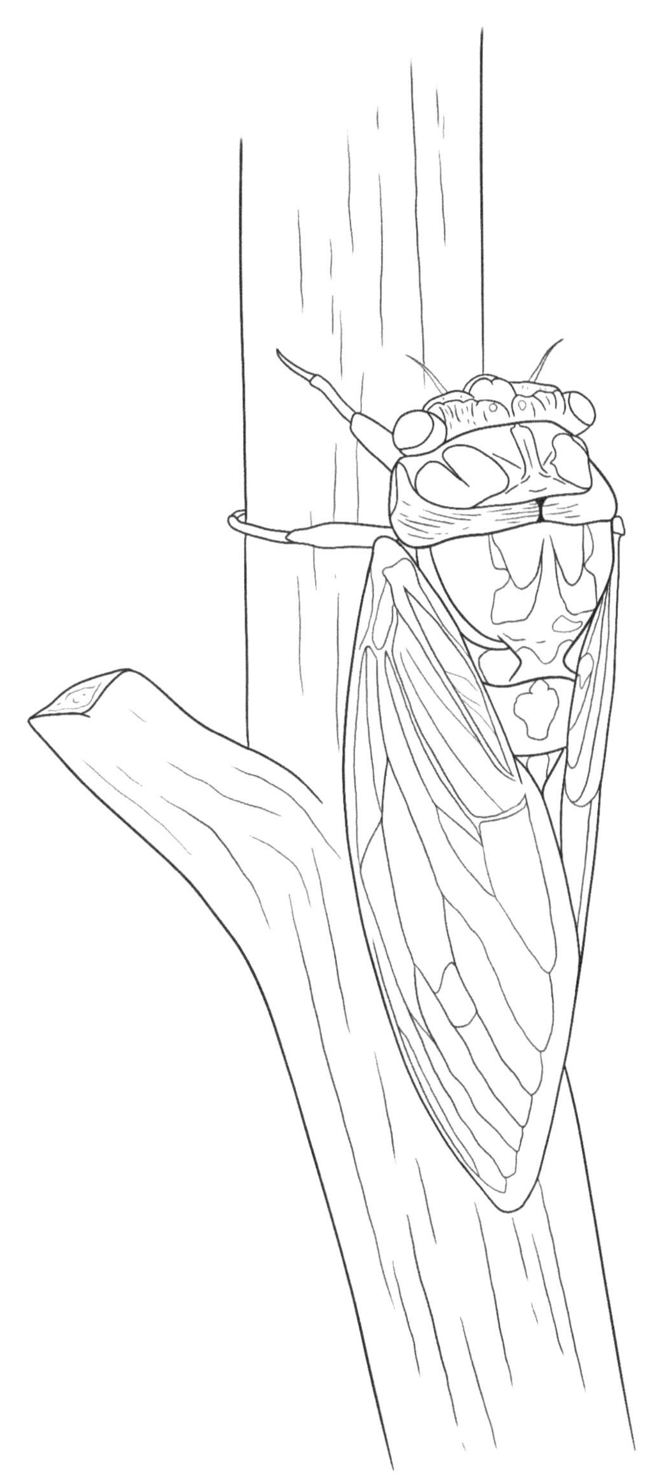

GARDEN SNAIL

Cornu aspersum

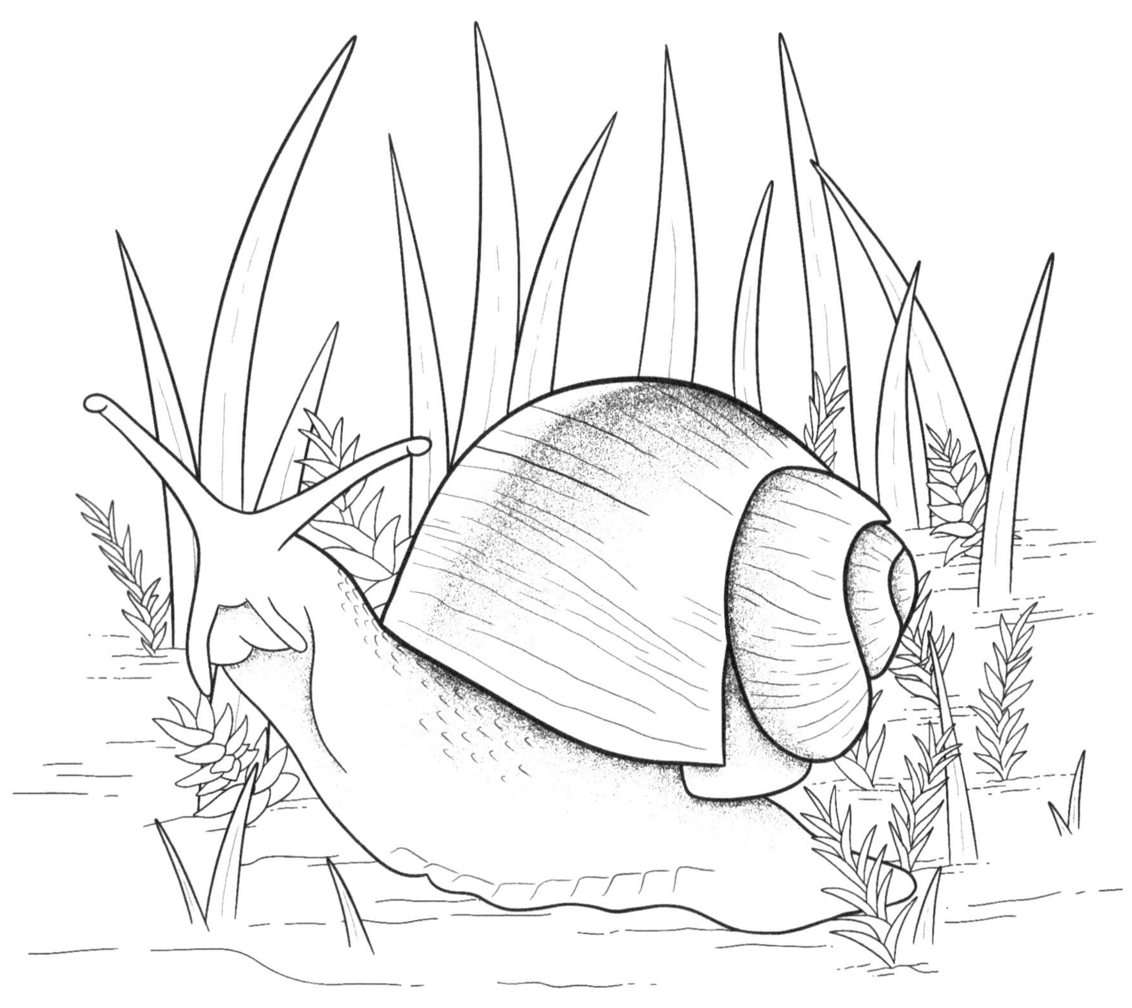

PIPEVINE SWALLOWTAIL

Battus philenor

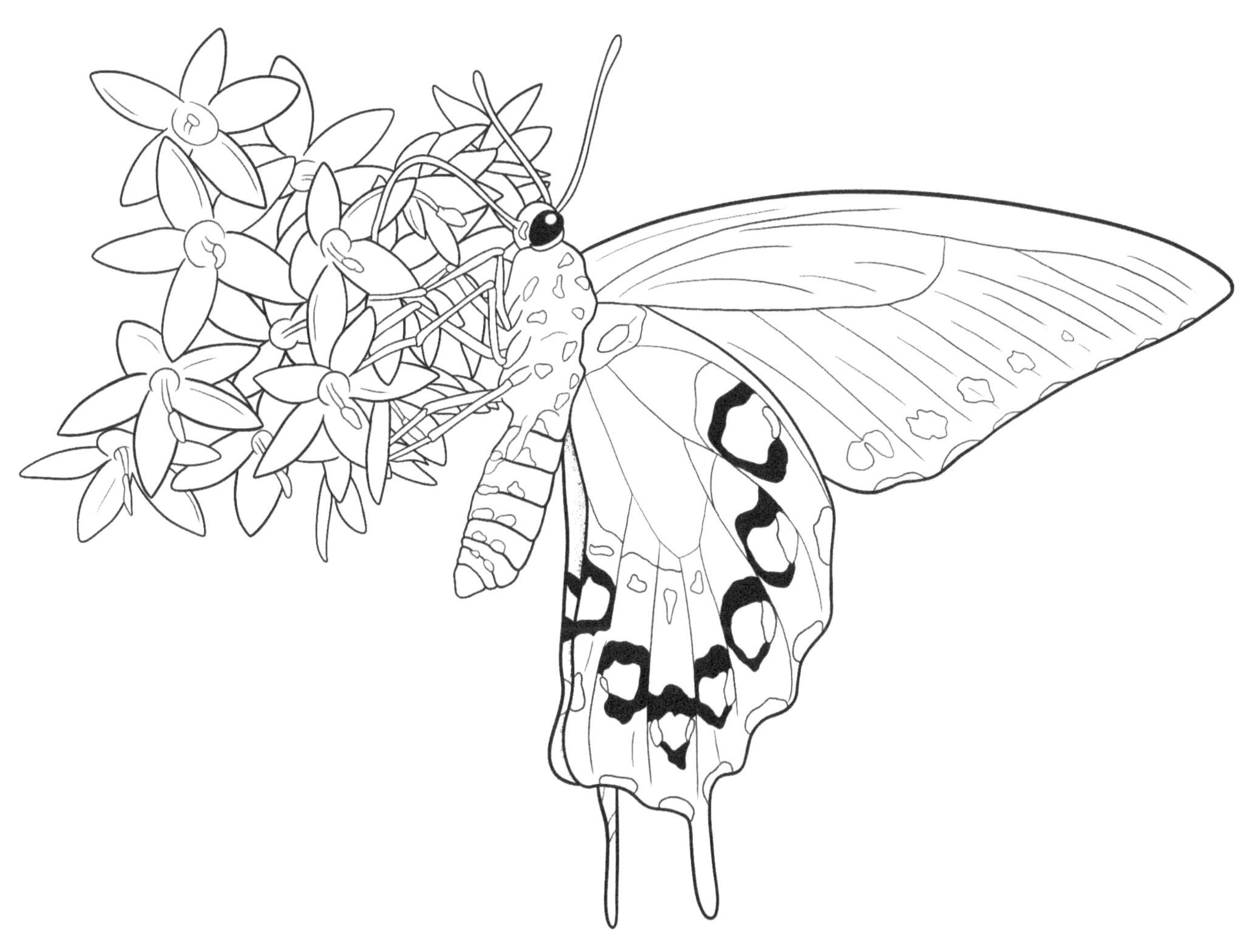

POTATO BEETLE

Leptinotarsa decemlineata

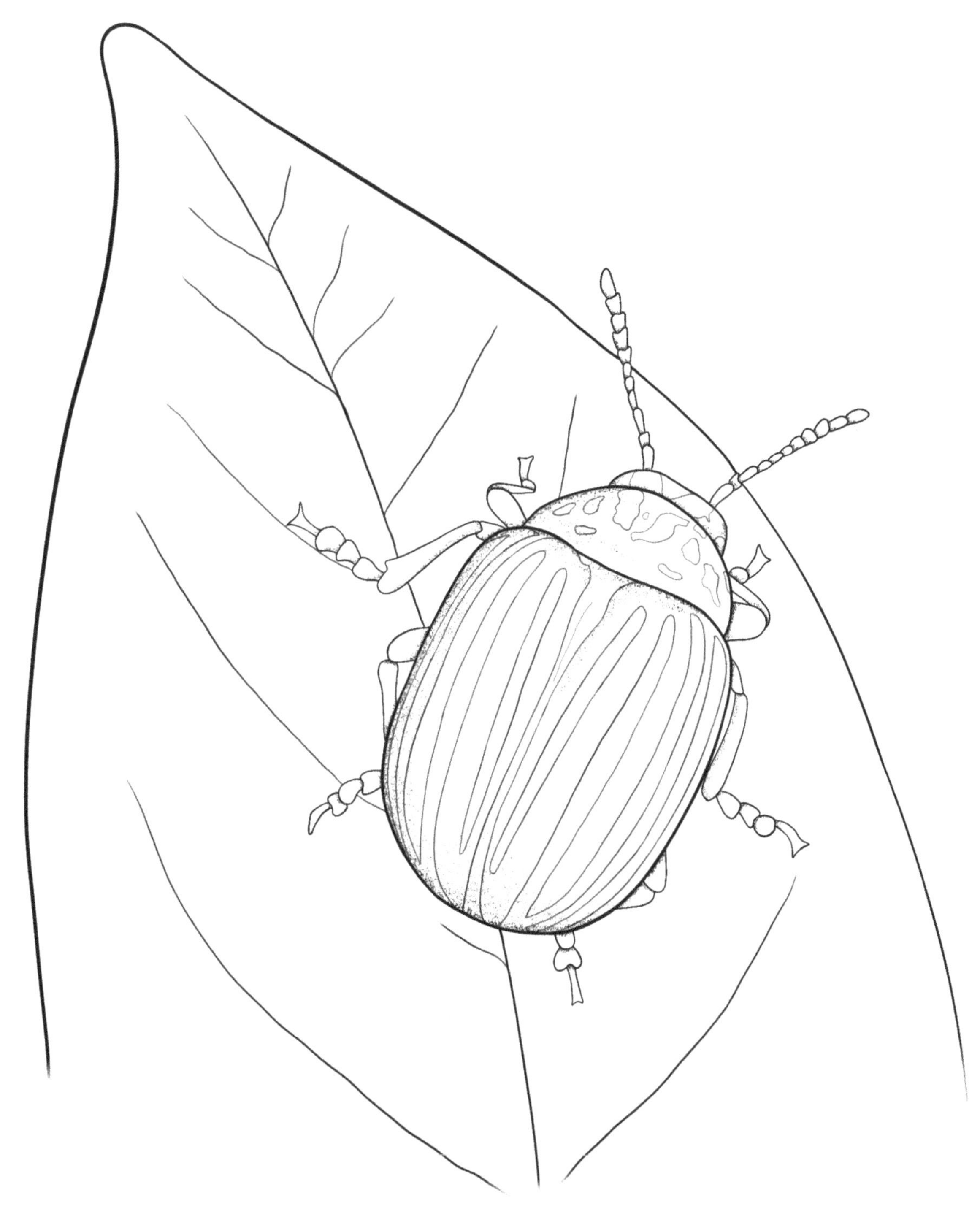

LARGE RED DAMSELFLY

Pyrrhosoma nymphula

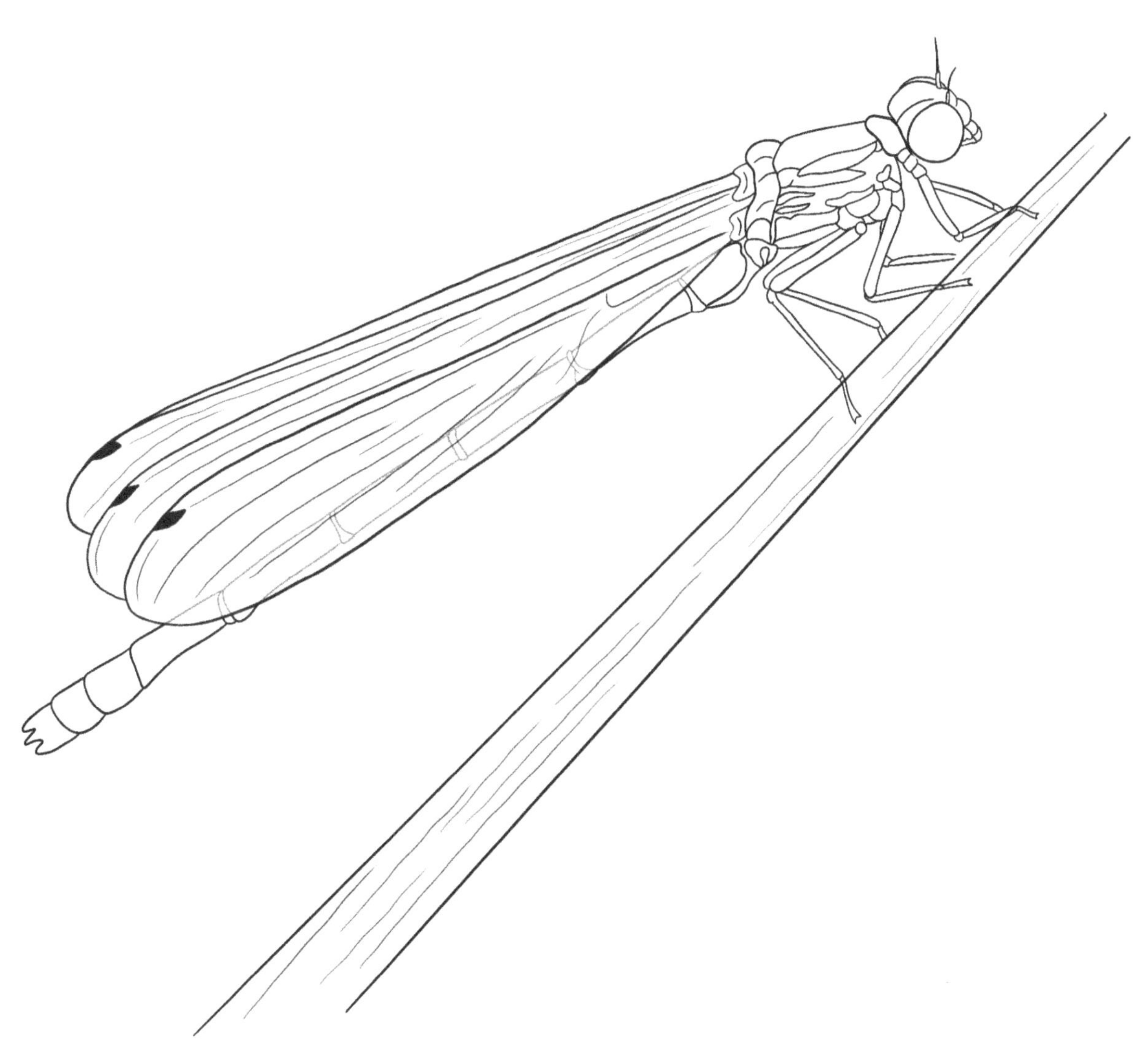

WOOD FROG
Lithobates sylvaticus

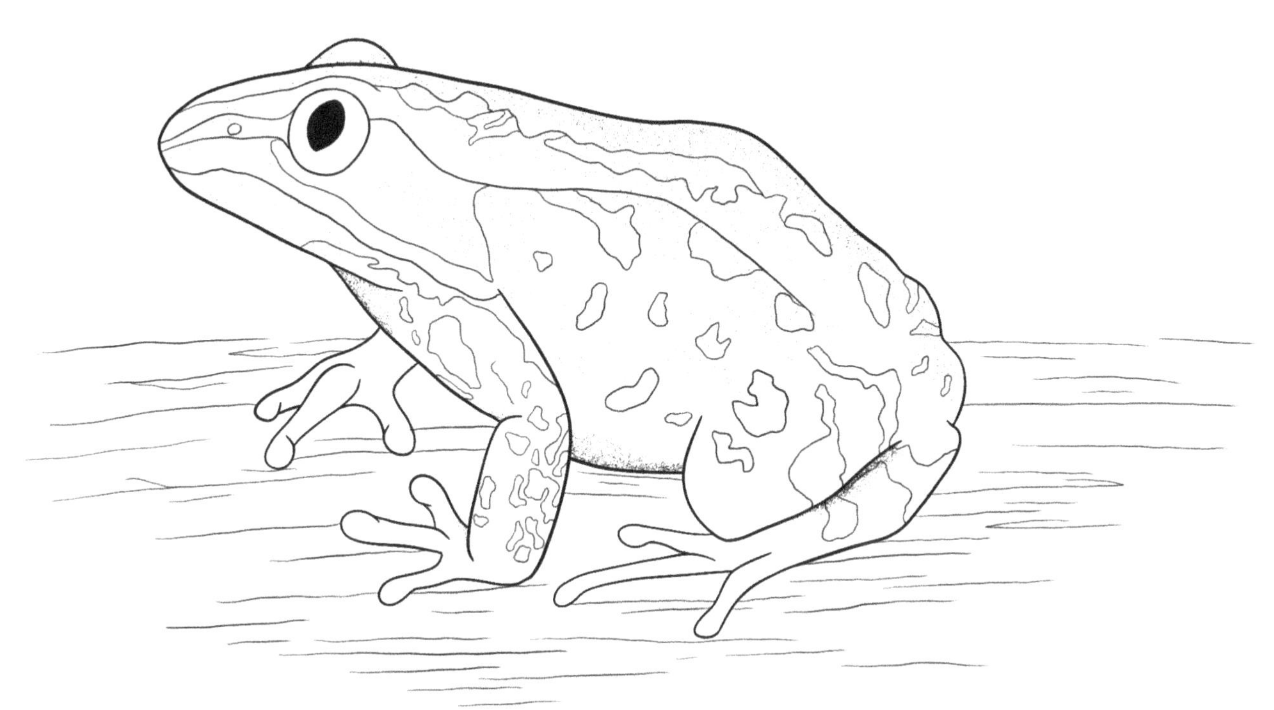

PEARL CRESCENT

Phyciodes tharos

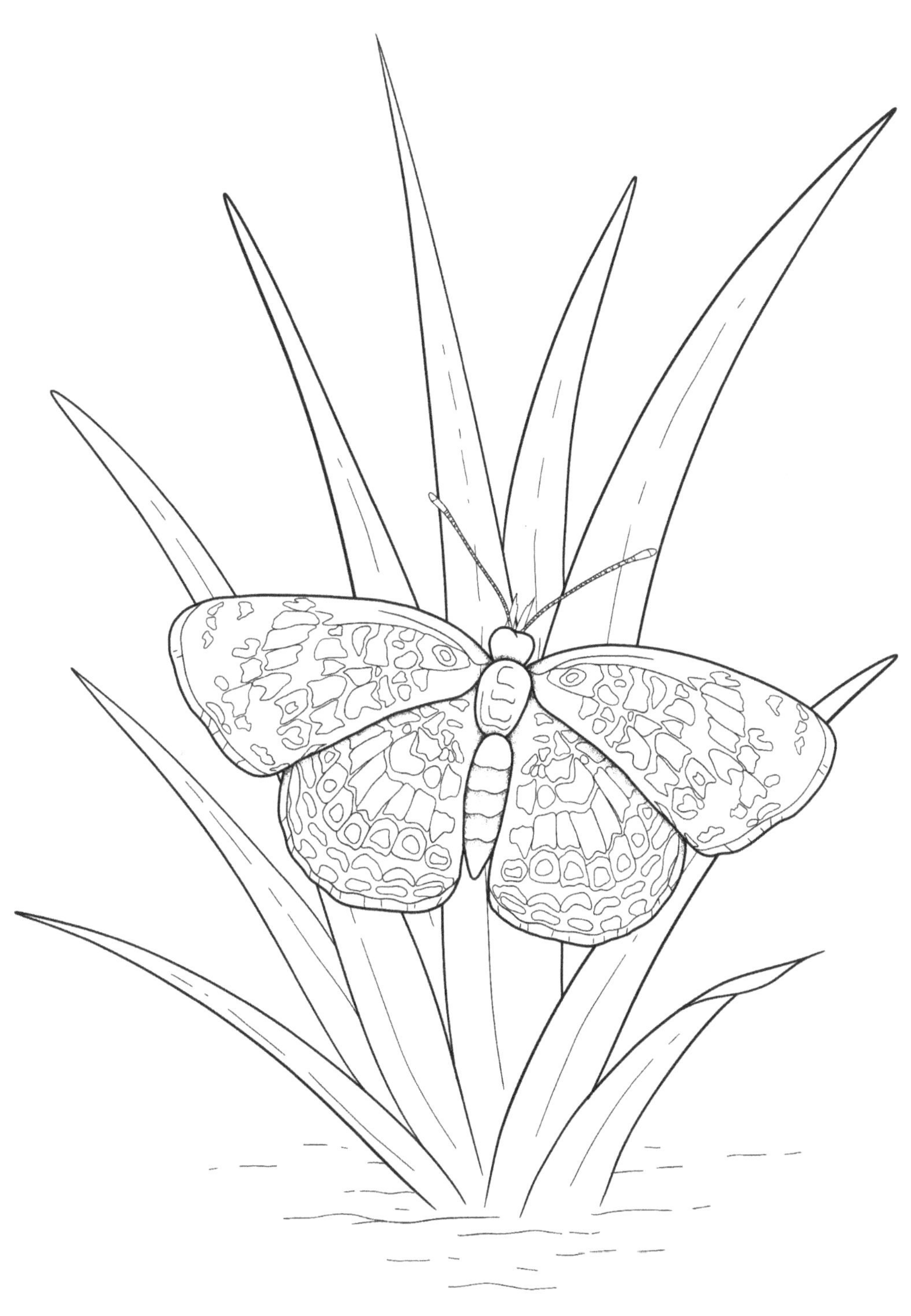

MANTIS
Mantodea

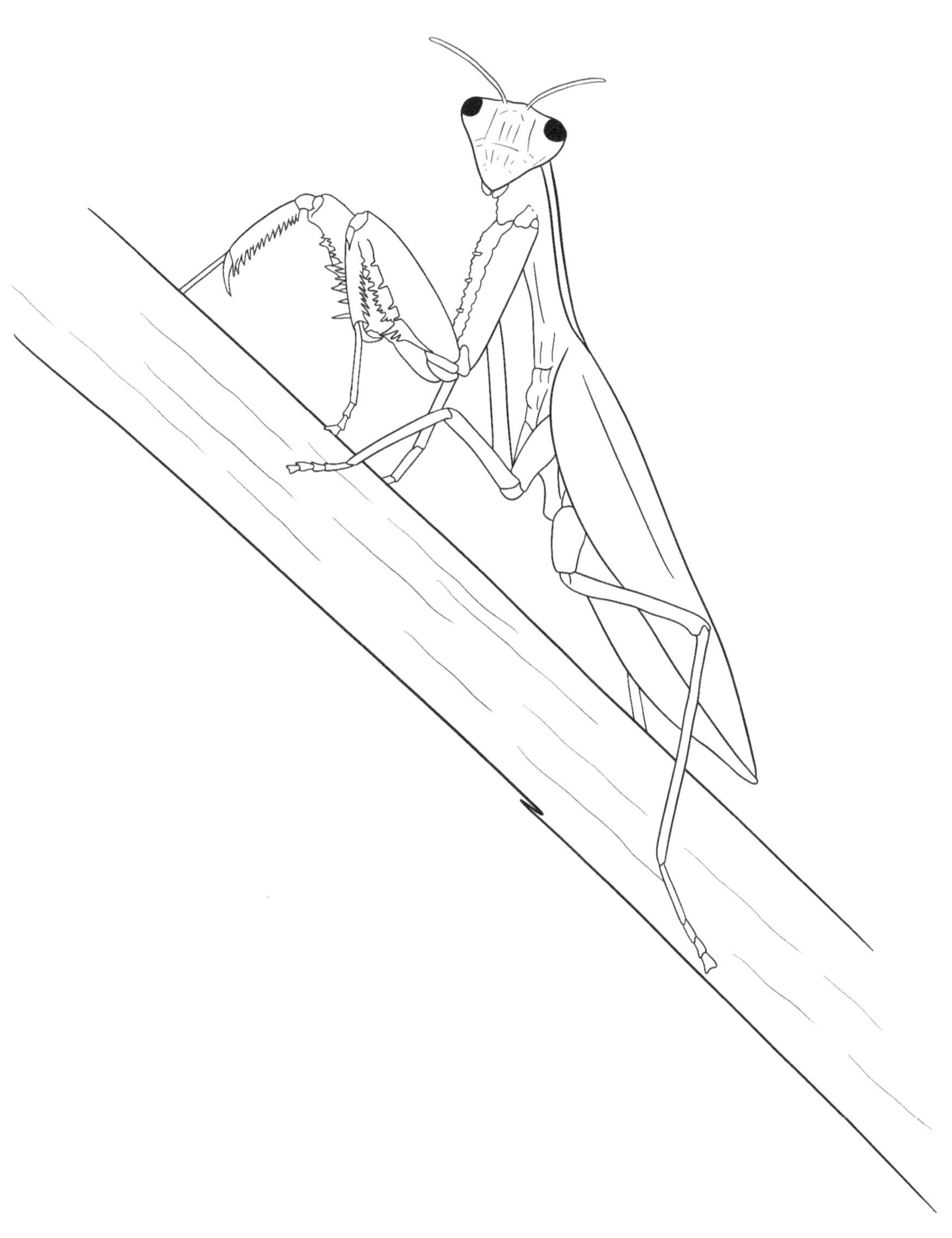

PAINTED TURTLE
Chrysemys picta

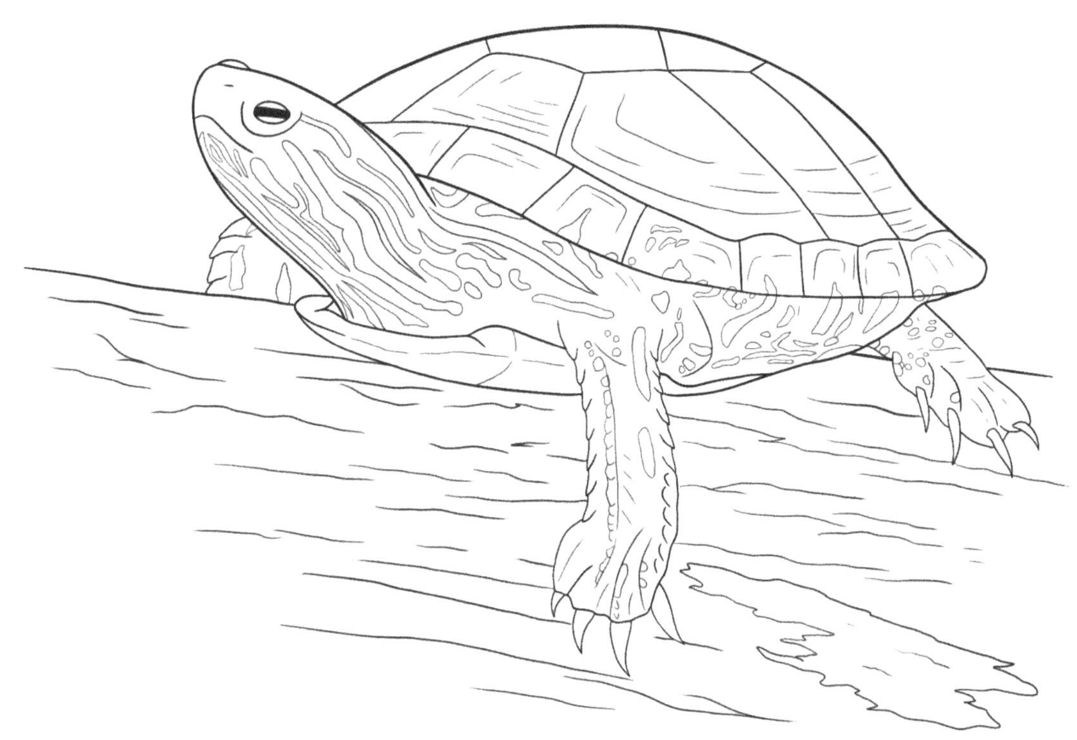

MONARCH BUTTERFLY
Danaus plexippus

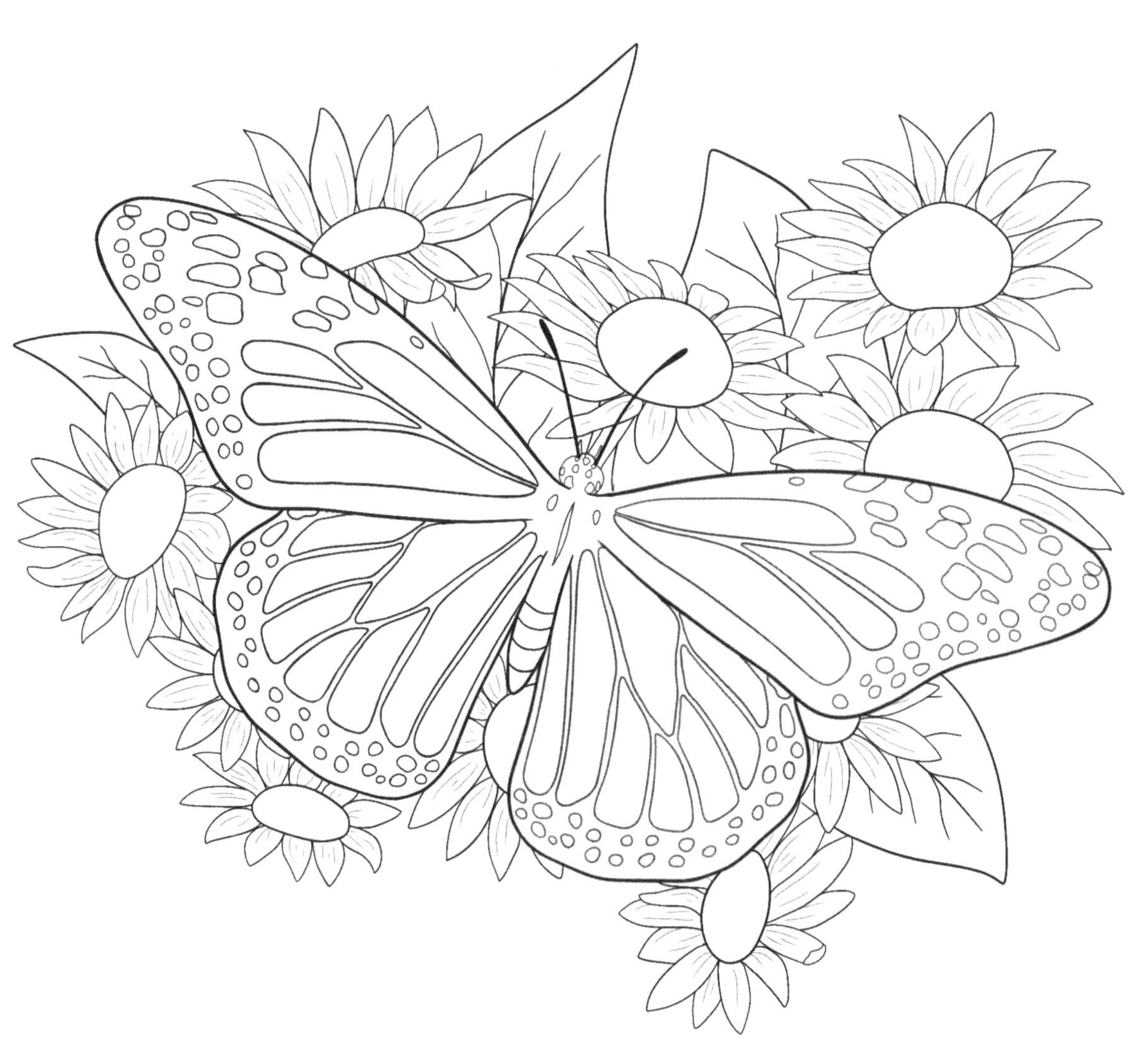

AMERICAN TOAD
Anaxyrus americanus

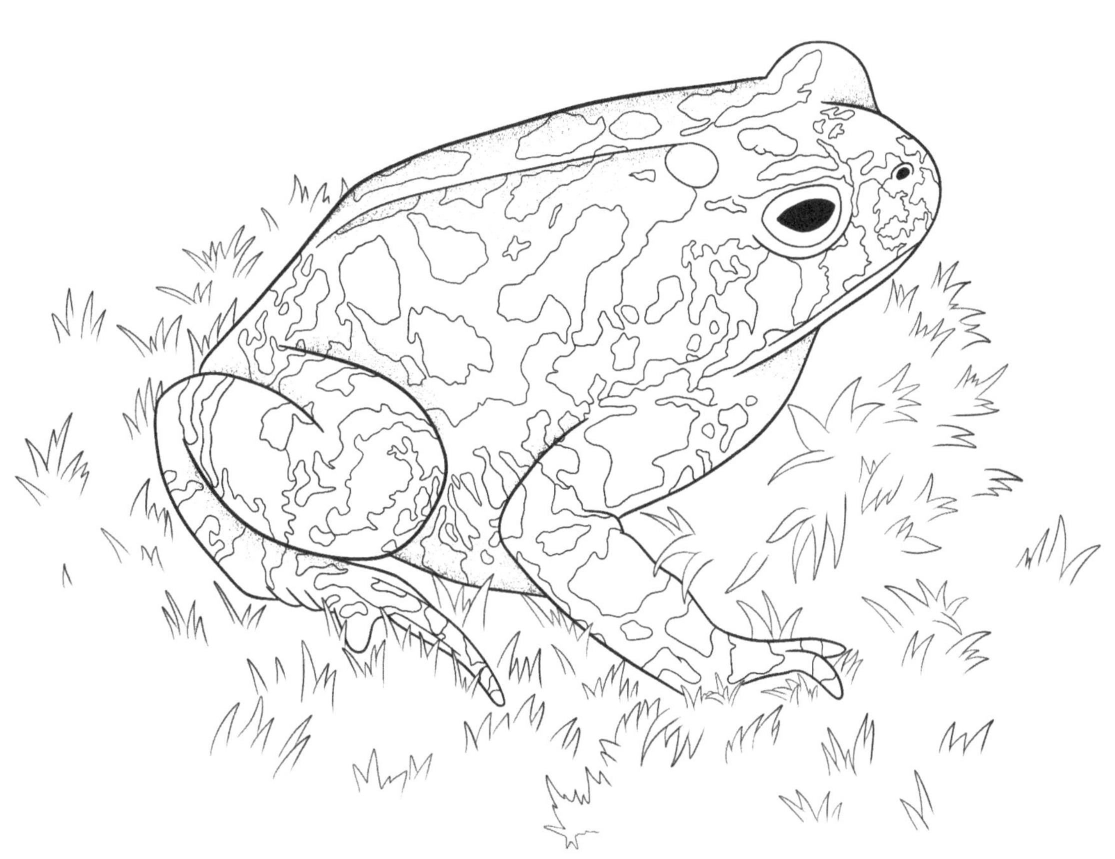

JUNE BEETLE
Cotinis nitida

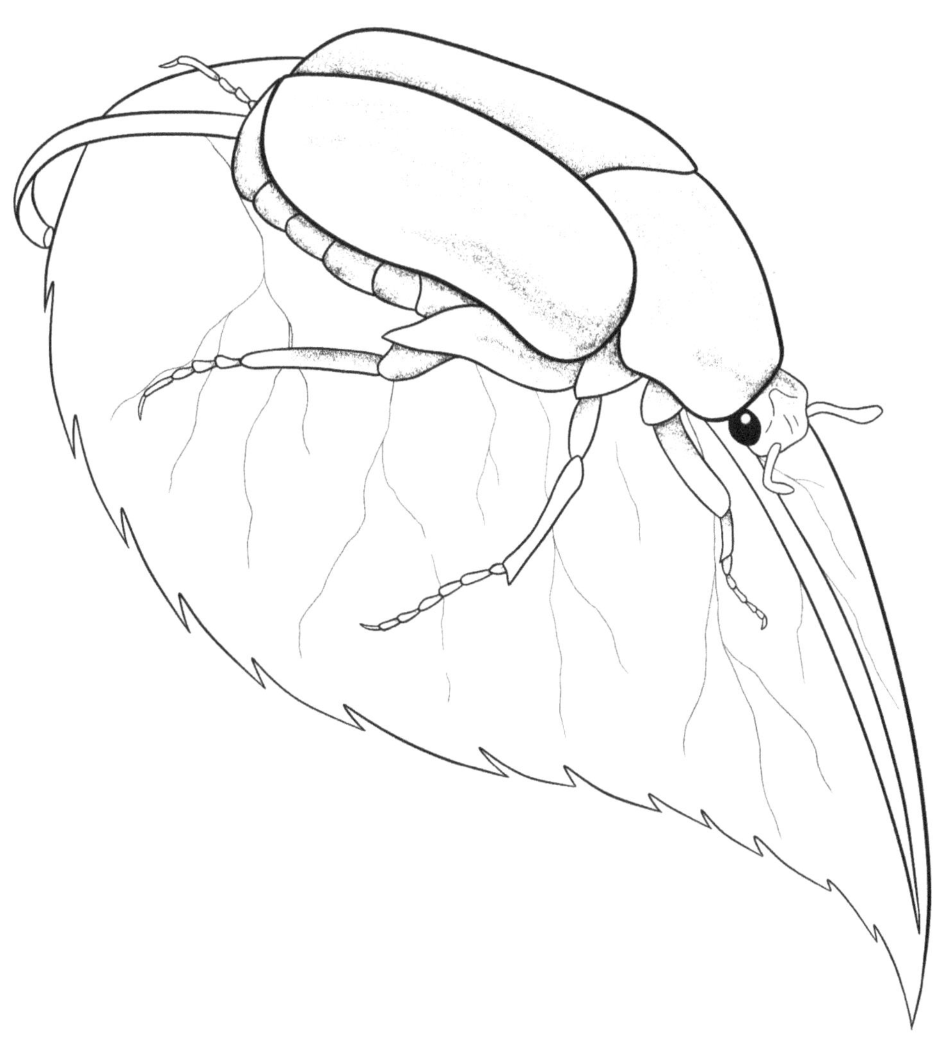

COMMON MEADOW KATYDID

Orchelimum vulgare

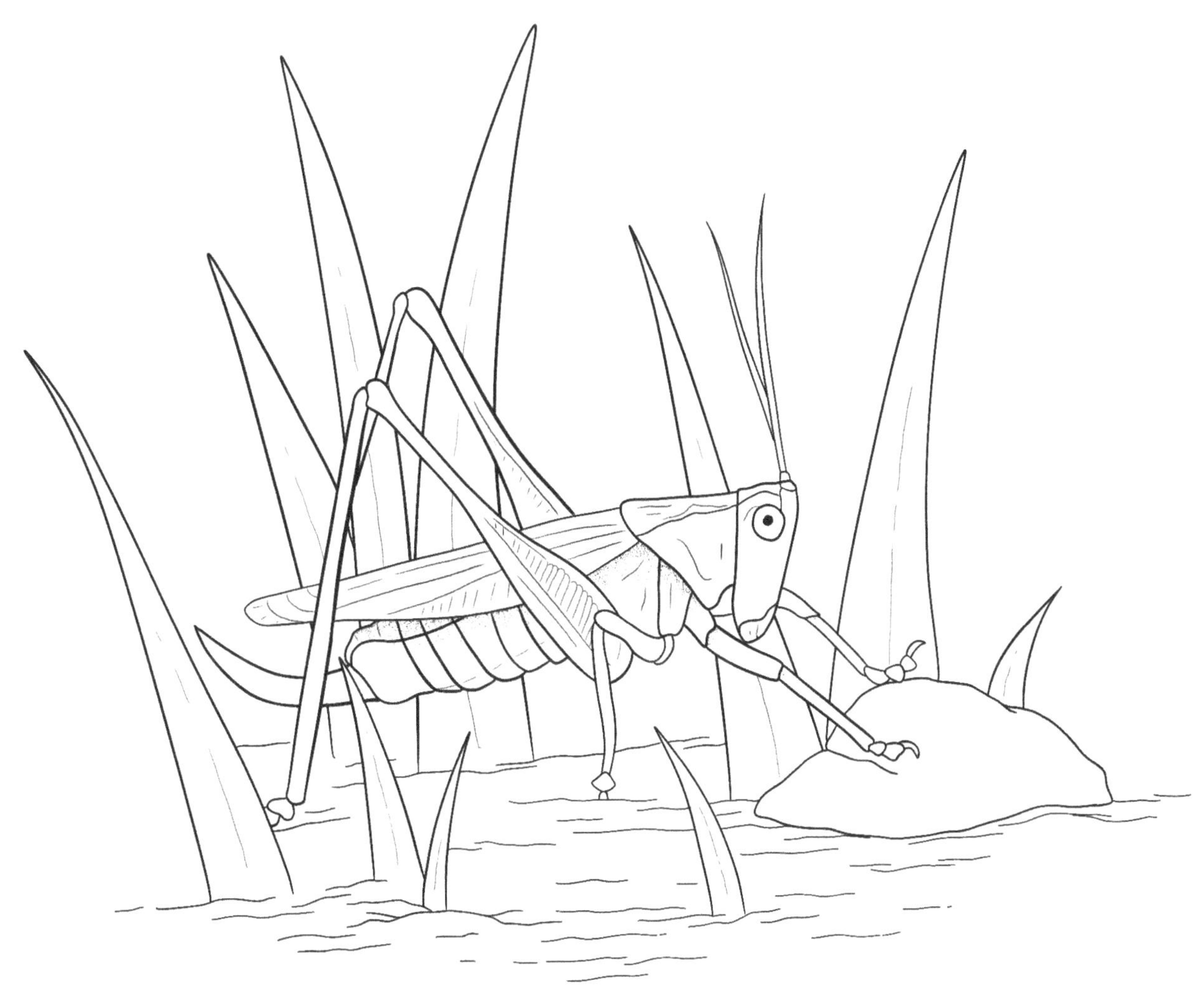

EMPEROR DRAGONFLY

Anax imperator

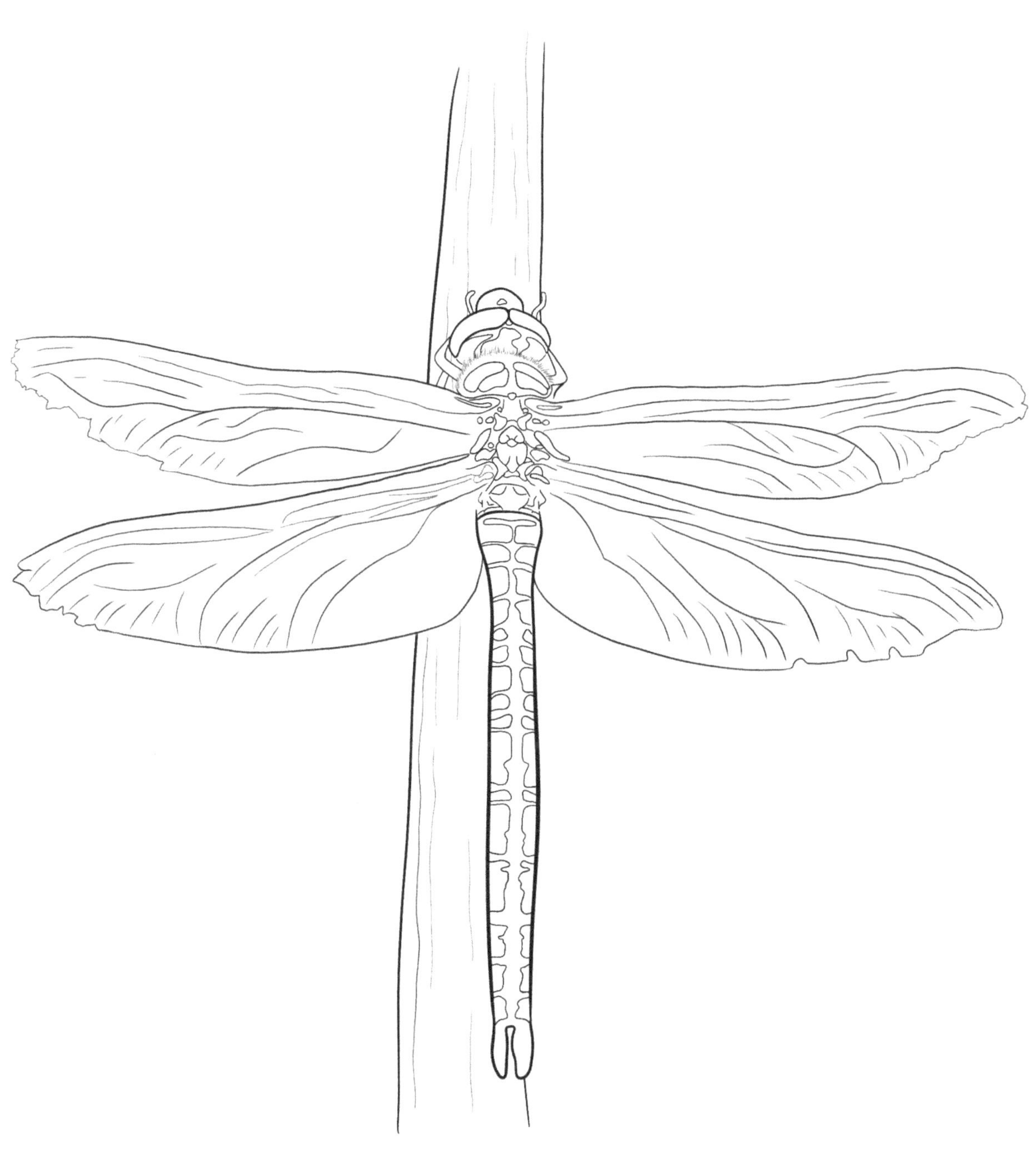

BULLFROG
Lithobates catesbeianus

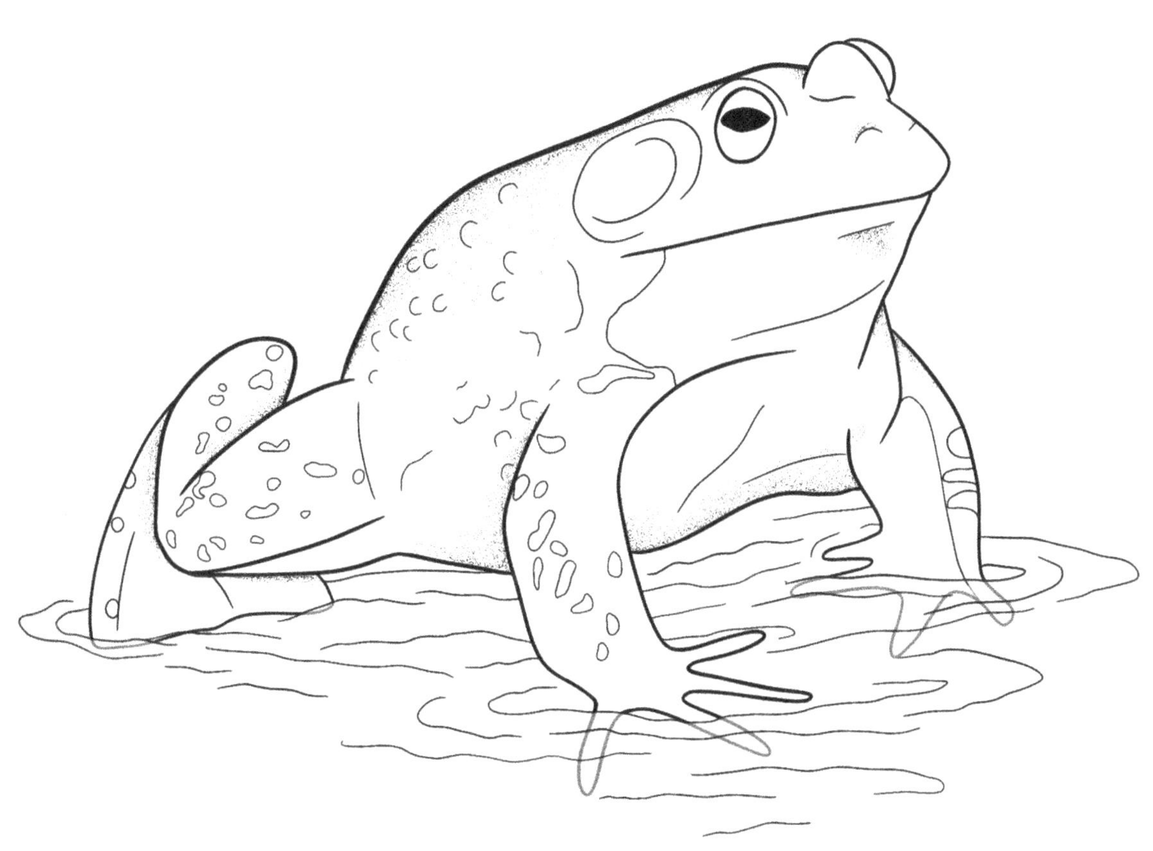

VIRGIN TIGER MOTH

Apantesis virgo

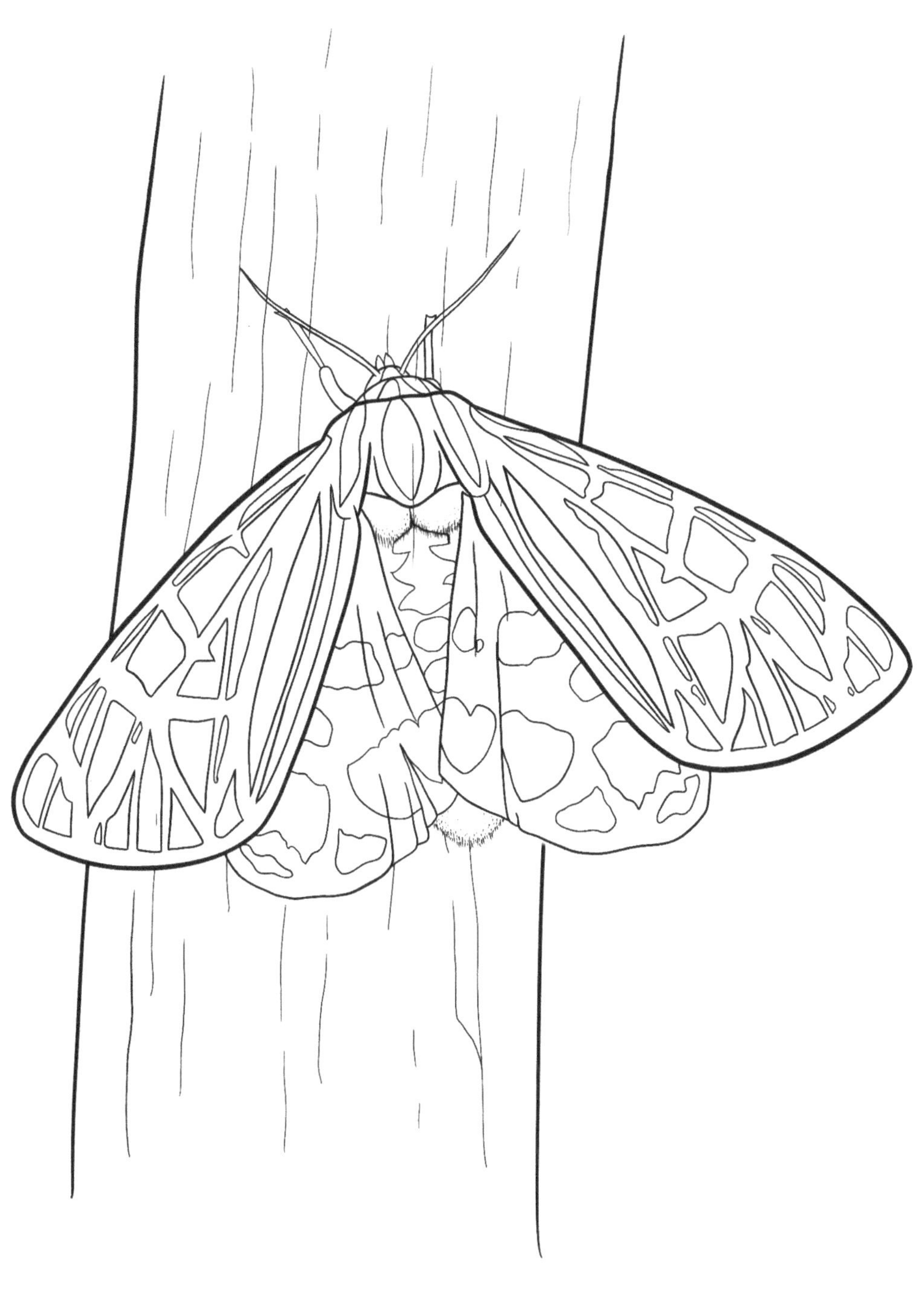

ROLY POLY
Armadillidium vulgare

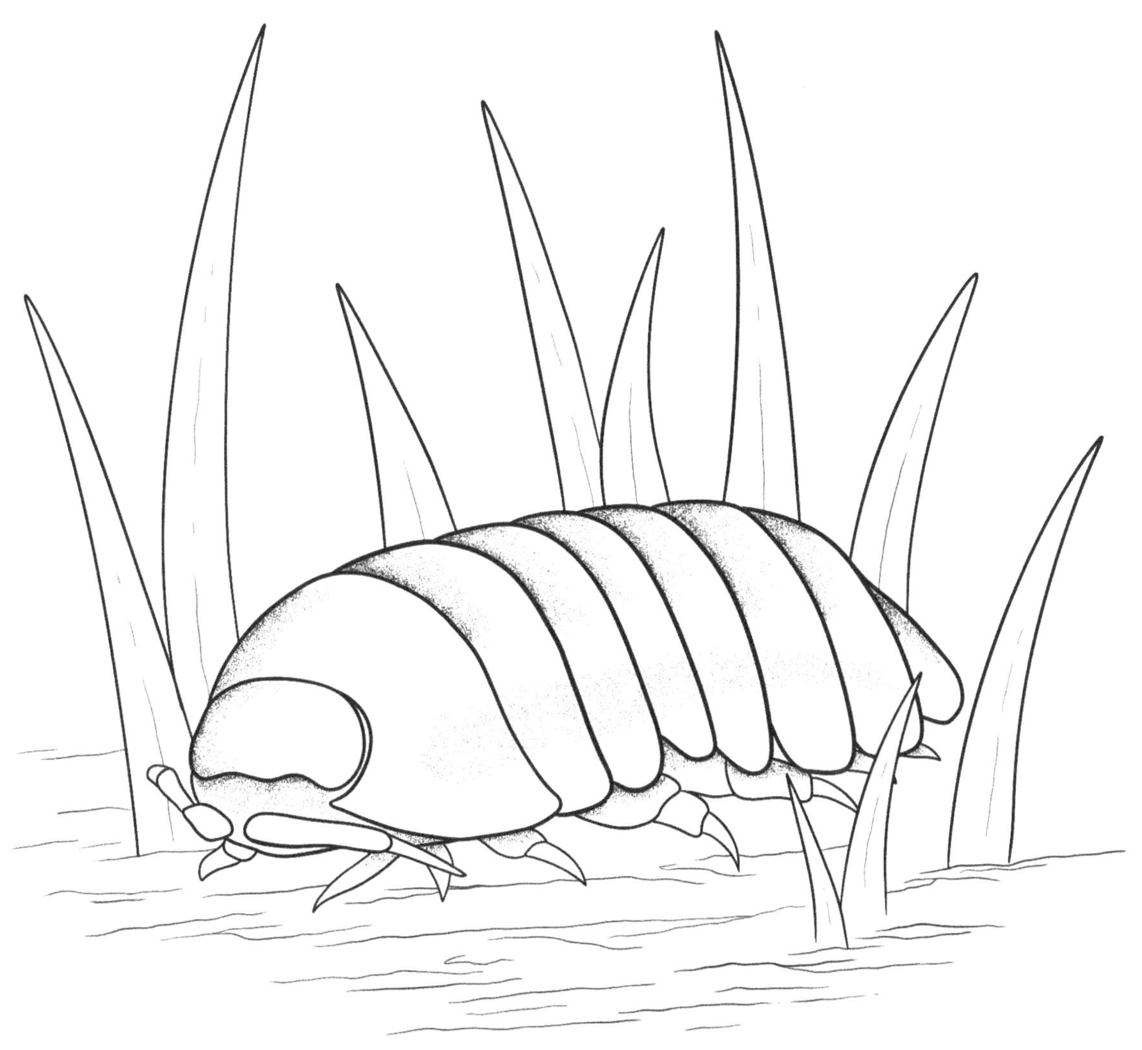

DIFFERENTIAL GRASSHOPPER
Melanoplus differentialis

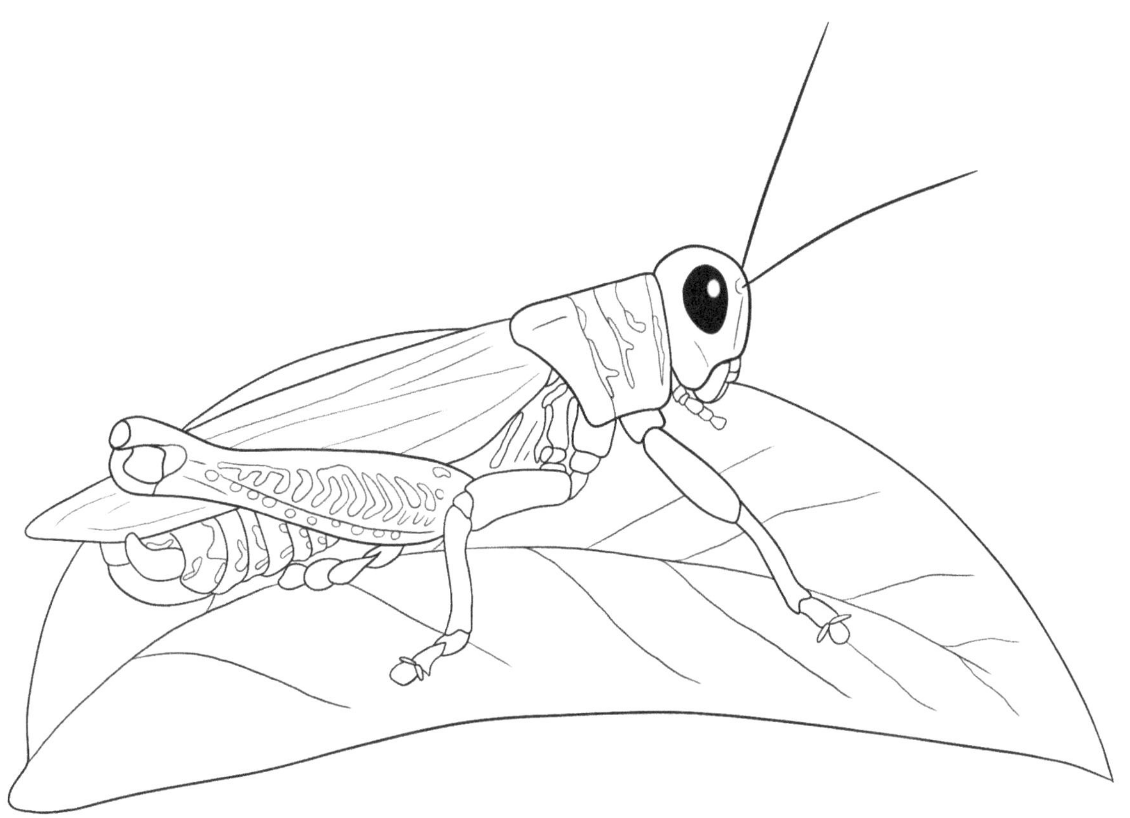